BOBBE
BAGGIO,
PH.D.

VIRTUAL
TOUCH
POINTS

LEADING, INSPIRING & MEASURING PERFORMANCE IN
THE VIRTUAL WORKPLACE

First Edition: 2017

ISBN: 978-0-9914051-1-4

LCCN: 2017958335

Ebook and Print Interior Design by Steven W. Booth,
      www.GeniusBookServices.com

Cover Design by Senhor Tocas, www.SenhorTocasIllustrator.tumblr.com

Table of Contents

Most people who work virtually love it. More people are demanding this as an option. Despite the efforts of companies like IBM, Yahoo, Bank of America, and Aetna to try to reverse course and pull the virtual workers back into the office, virtual work is a trend that will not roll back. Mostly for control issues and out of desperation, companies try to turn back time. Workers are having none of it. Smart companies are not either. Depending on the source, 40% or more of the workforce is currently working virtually. The number of days, hours or some other criteria often qualifies this. What is undeniable though is that this number is growing.

In 2015, IBM boasted that 40% of its work force was virtual and that it had the tools and systems to support this trend. Surveys conducted by Gallop support 20% of the workforce works virtually full time and about 43% works virtually some of the time. Many giants like United Healthcare, Salesforce.com, American Express and Amazon support a virtual workplace. Virtual work is desirable, improves the quality of life and allows for work-life balance and autonomy. Do not interpret this incorrectly, it has its challenges. Nevertheless, consistently, it cuts cost for both the employee and the employer, increases employee satisfaction and retention, and broadens recruiting circles (Simons, 2017).

The bigger picture is that most companies do not know what to do with the virtual workforce. They are not sure how to lead, inspire, or measure performance. With a workforce spread across the globe and teams in different time zones and on different continents, synchronous and asynchronous communication is critical. The tools currently available and coming are making virtual work more accessible to more people. The tools are getting better but a company's ability to provide these tools varies. They help employees communicate with new paths and easy access. Virtual employees can travel in the same connection circles, like walking down the hall to the old water cooler. Organizations that support virtual workers tend to be flatter (less hierarchical), more inspiring and more inclusionary. They are more open to innovation and more interested in results.

What is more interesting is the overall inability of organizations to define knowledge work and performance measures. Mutually agreed upon objectives and clear consistent communication is critical. Collaboration and team building are vital to success in the virtual workplace. All of these success factors take effort. Some workplace roles and some human abilities lend themselves to remote work more than others. HR, engineering, software development, data science, analytics, transaction processing, research and development (R&D), sales, customer support in industries from medical records to insurance to consulting are natural jobs for the virtual workplace. Granted, some jobs do not fit the bill but many do.

Success in the virtual workplace requires leadership that is committed to making it work. Leaders need to understand and be willing to support virtual workers. Leadership needs to invest in and believe that this is an inevitable workplace transformation. When the virtual workplace is supported well by leadership, they do not have morale issues, cultural repercussions or experience exclusion. People are engaged, included and welcomed into the company and appreciated for their contributions to the organization's overall success. When leaders support the virtual workplace, they are willing to be transparent. They are willing to set clear expectations and have clearly defined processes. They are willing to be open, honest and inclusive in defining performance, which is the difference between transparency and visibility. The virtual workplace is here to stay. It is time for companies to stop making excuses and get on board with making it work because it benefits everyone as well as the planet.

Introduction

Work is not what it used to be. The workplace of the present is not the workplace of even a few years ago. The workplace has experienced enormous change in expectations, structure, content and process. Work is more cognitively demanding, team based, virtual, dependent on technology, and less restricted by time and place. This affects the worker and the organization. The worker is expected to know more and be willing to continually learn, grow and change. The work itself is more complex and demanding. It requires new ways of thinking, constantly adapting and innovating. Workers interact differently with each other and with the organization. The organization has also changed. It is less secure, leaner, more customer oriented and flatter. The new workplace has increased time burdens, different rules and less boundaries. All of this has put enormous pressure on leaders to understand how technology has changed the workplace.

Flexible work arrangements including virtual work and flexible hours are something that workers are demanding. Workers have less long-term loyalty and more psychological self-determination. They want to participate, be appreciated, and have an identity and self-expression. Long-term organizational commitment, job security and lifelong careers are outdated. With flatter organizations, there are less guarantees and more opportunities to move between organizations.

Asking people to work with autonomy is asking people to be independent. Workers today value improved quality of work-life balance and the attraction of new learning opportunities. Organizations have to learn to lead, inspire and measure human performance in a virtual work environment. This new workplace is here to stay.

Many companies have tried to turn back time, but the virtual workplace continues to grow. Most people who work virtually say they will never go back to the office full time. They get so much more done working virtually. Chapter 1 discusses the impact technology has had on the worker and the work place. There are many challenges to the new workplace. Innovative ideas, creative thinking and trust are needed to create an environment that supports productivity.

The impact new technology has on individuals and organizational culture is immense. This constant and continuing change requires ongoing adjustments. All this change is disruptive and disturbing both to the individual and to organizations. Technological disruption shakes the very core of organizational power and control.

Virtual workers struggle with invisibility and organizations struggle with perceived loss of control and trust. Virtual relationships require communicating in different ways, ways that support both the individual and the organizational objectives and goals. Part of the challenge of the new workplace is managing the invisible and learning to listen in new ways.

Effective communication improves performance success in virtual environments. Maximizing the effectiveness of communication is discussed in Chapter 2. Patterns of communication learned in childhood often influence us well into adulthood, often in ways that are not supportive or productive. This chapter also talks about the importance of trust in virtual environments. The virtual workplace is impacted by the trust workers have in other team members, the trust they have in leadership, and the

Leading in a Virtual Environment

trust they have in the processes and technologies that supports their goals.

Many organizations are caught up in a culture of control. Culture manifests itself in organizations in many ways. Chapter 3 discusses the "illusion of control" and how influence and control in a virtual environment come about in very different ways. The importance of recognizing implicit biases and releasing stereotypes is discussed. Stereotyping is depersonalizing and controlling behavior that reinforces patterns and beliefs that are not helpful to the individual or the organization. Understanding the current culture and how it can be supportive through innovation and creativity is a dramatic change for many organizations.

Effective communication and the importance of intuitive listening are discussed in Chapter 4. Listening in the virtual environment requires different and enhanced skills. The four levels of listening are active listening, reflective listening, responsive listening and intuitive listening. Active listening requires focus and attention. It is the first step to tuning in to people. Reflective listening is a technique used to acknowledge the speaker and confirm your understanding of the message. You reflect, or check your understanding of what is being said by mirroring or restating what you have heard. Responsive listening takes active listening one step farther. Responsive listening changes the dynamics and opens doors to establishing new connections and relationships. Responsive listening validates autonomy and inspires intuitive listening. Intuitive listening confirms the importance of a person's intentions and alignment. Intuitive listening allows for eavesdropping between the lines and determining what message is really being conveyed.

Chapter 5 gives you a method to communicate that establishes FROG, (family, recreation, occupation and goals) as a technique for connecting to the individual. FROG, when used with tact and discretion, can open doors to new relationships and build solid foundations. FROG helps to build trust and cement engagement. FROG can help dissolve the alienation and isolation of working in a virtual environment. Chapter 5 also discusses ways people make mistakes when trying to make human connections including the traps many of us fall into. For example, telling and not asking is a common mistake.

The X factor is about human intuition. Intuition has historically played an important role in leadership. Logic and analytics have taken a front and center role in how people lead, but often what we say and what we really do are not the same thing. Intuition and trust go hand in hand. Chapter 6 discusses how to use your intuition to lead in a virtual environment and Chapter 7 discusses the importance of leadership supplying support through proactive collaborating, communicating and sharing.

Chapter 8 initiates the measurement of human performance in virtual work environments. It discusses performance appraisals (PA) and turnover rates. The importance of mutually agreed upon success measures and what questions might help in determining appropriate and measurable performance is covered. It also discusses what happens when virtual teams or individuals have issues with leadership and turn against their leaders. Trust again is at the heart of the matter, and when virtual teams mutiny it is usually because this trust has been violated.

Inspiring Performance in the Virtual Workplace

Measuring Performance in the Virtual Environment

Chapters 9 and 10 cover the challenges and opportunities to measure performance in a virtual environment. The virtual workplace requires a redefinition of what we call performance and new and innovative ways to measure it. It requires leadership to communicate a vision then getting buy-in for that vision as well as engagement to accomplish that vision. Performance measurement is a process that requires setting individual, learning and strategic objectives. It requires more than an annual performance evaluation. In a virtual work environment, performance analysis is an ongoing process. Performance analytics require evaluating the processes, systems, technology and culture that support the individuals. Evaluating performance requires much more than checking off boxes or filling in Likert scales. Performance analysis in the virtual workplace is about planning, training and adjusting.

Finally, the last chapter discusses opportunities for improvement. Performance analysis is about comparing where we are to where we want to be. This is true on an individual, department and organizational level. Clear expectations, benchmarks and accountability are important. Opportunities to improve the virtual environment will come about because of our ability to track and use data of all sorts and varieties. With big data comes big responsibilities and it is important to be part of the crucial conversations about virtual performance measurement. When we measure personal performance it needs to be transparent and responsible. There are excellent opportunities for companies to evolve the virtual workplace to an environment that optimizes performance for the individual and the organization.

Leading in a Virtual Environment

There has been a significant shift in the workplace in the last decade toward "intellectual capital" and a reframing of the role of manager as one of leader. Gone are the days of being able to tell if a worker is a good one because he or she spends exorbitant amounts of time behind the desk. The age of the knowledge worker ushered in a time of "knowing," an era when what was important was in your mind not on the assembly line. Good soldiers, you see, were broken. Their independence sacrificed for the cause. Their intellectual spark vanished because they lost something important in the battle of control. They lost their ability to think and act with autonomy. They lost the ability to think for themselves.

In many organizations, leadership is lost. They have little or no idea how to inspire and measure performance in the virtual world. They are lost in a paradigm of the past, one that says management should influence and control. In the virtual world, in contrast, it is essential for the individual to be authentically productive. The real reason people get called back to the office is not one of collaboration and inspiration but one of trust. When workers are not in a face to face environment, leadership is not sure how to tap into the creativity, innovation and productivity of their workforce. It is not the economy, business cycle, outsourcing or offshoring that is the problem. It is lack of individual support and empowerment. Manage comes from a root word that is the same as the one used for "manipulate" or "maneuver," and means to change something to fit a purpose. The image of the good soldier willing to sacrifice everything for the cause is still alive in some organizations. However, even in corporate cultures long known for this, the mentality is beginning to

Chapter 1

Managing the Invisible

Technology is not technology if it happened before you were born.
—Sir Ken Robinson

change. Power is the ability to act with autonomy. To create and innovate you need the freedom to act without judgment.

Innovation in many organizations has become as extinct as Tyrannosaurus rex. This is really a dilemma in a world of constant change. Success seems to depend on adapting to the new. Some organizations are waking up to the need to empower people. This requires inspiring them to think for themselves so that they can respond creatively to the relentless change that surrounds them. Other are still operating in a fear-based mentality. They are afraid of what they cannot see. They are afraid of losing control and afraid of the soldiers deserting. The Harvard Business Review writes books about innovation and the Economist runs articles on creativity. But what really needs to happen will not be created by essay. It will be inspired by technology and the freedom inherent in the virtual environment.

Technology gives us the ability to be independent yet connected. You can be at basketball practice in a high school gym in Philadelphia and have a meeting with someone in Japan. If you have a cellphone, tablet or a laptop and a connection you can engage in global commerce. Access to world markets is easy. Organizations are starting to understand that managing people that work in this detached but connected environment might require a new approach.

Created by Technology

Businesses and organizations are using technology exponentially to communicate and organize "Big Data." The hope is that the organization can impact the bottom line either by lowering costs or driving revenue. Technology provides opportunities to respond to global markets and create new relationships that may be advantageous. Technology allows people to interact, engage and share experiences without being physically together. This ability to interact without physical presence is what happens in the virtual environment. These new environments exist because they can.

Changes fueled by an unlimited technology arsenal impact our relationships at work. Consultants, micro workers and experts are available to organizations. A global workforce at your fingertips provides both speed and reach. Compensation practices, the layout of the workplace and job expectations are under scrutiny. Organizations are rethinking what "good looks like." They are attempting to break down silos (isolation), embrace and not limit vacations, have casual days every day and share visions. This technology is also disruptive and has the impact of changing not only where we work but how.

The virtual workplace is here. People rely on electronic communication and virtual connectivity to get their jobs done. This reliance on technology has created an environment that has a double edge. You are both isolated and constantly connected. More than 50 million people travel less but work just as effectively using technology. They don't have to be in the office and they don't need to travel for meetings either. To some extent this technology has been liberating. People don't have to do long commutes, sit in traffic or fight the weather. They can work at home in their "pajamas" if they choose. The new environment is a more relaxed, less structured and more flexible environment than the traditional workplace. Remote access with web-based technology, collaboration tools and smart devices supports flexible work environments and adaptive schedules. It also appears to be flatter.

You can have a direct connection to higher levels of management. These people, who were unapproachable in the face to face (F2F) world, are a Tweet or an email away. But there is another much darker and disturbing side to the virtual environment. It is an environment of paradoxes, of opposites and of contradictions. Authority, authenticity, privacy, accountability and identity are only a few of the dichotomies facing the virtual workplace. The old structures are falling but slowly. Like the coliseum in Rome, position, rewards and recognition from another time are still standing in many organizations.

Not All That Flat

Personal devices give us the impression of one to one communication. Research as far back as the 1960s on human to computer interactions reinforces the fact that we like to relate to devices in a one to one, personal way. We relate to the device as if we were talking to another human being, which sometimes we are and sometimes we are not. It is an illusion that since we adopted social networks everyone one is on the same level and everyone is accessible. After all, we can receive personal "Tweets" from rock stars, presidential candidates and football heroes. Authority, however, is still an issue in most organizations. The hierarchy, the chain of command, salary structures and corporate ladders are remnants from a different time and are just starting to be phased out. Collaboration is now disrupted by an old paradigm of authority and power. Speed and access are a part of this. The ability to collaborate or reach and create relationships with other people is also an influence on organizational change. Value in the virtual workplace is created through connections with others.

Power formerly came from hierarchy, position and compensation. The virtual workplace reduces barriers to entry and achievement. Organizational rituals like F2F meetings and sitting in the "power positions" at the heads of the table or right across from the boss are archaic and outdated in the virtual environment. The traditional ways of relating through control, influence and intimidation just don't work here. The job descriptions of the past also don't work, and that makes organizations very nervous. In the virtual environment, there are no corner offices, executive restrooms or preferred parking spaces. Many leadership, innovation and change management theories are obsolete in this new era. These models are derived from paradigms of the past. Without the benefits of charisma and immediate authority, it becomes less about structure and progression and more about availability and opportunity.

Working relationships tend to take on a new meaning when there are no traditional delineators of power. Authentic productivity and contributions are what count. The traditional chain of command and authority is being challenged. Working in the virtual world tests more than giving up collaboration at the water cooler. It challenges organizations to replace power based on charisma and authority with power based on expertise and contribution. We are changing not only how we manage but what we manage. We used to manage people, now we manage results.

Virtual work environments shine a light on the competing values of yesterday and today. Many organizations are reluctant to change. They are content with power networks and visibility that can demand recognition and reward. Traditional notions of executive power and hierarchy are part of Western culture. Most of what is written and researched about virtual teams is based on antiquated team theory from the last century. This is revisited and updated in a flawed attempt to reflect the virtual environment.

It is a challenge for human beings to integrate the new without reference to the context of the old. The virtual environment with all its side shows, big data, constant connectivity, global reach and boundless everything creates a very different challenge for leadership. Virtual teams are flatter and they cut across silos and infrastructures. For the last thirty years, organizations have looked to teams to increase performance. Virtual teams are more flexible, creative and fluent. They get a great deal of work done. Technology enables the transition to a virtual work environment, and virtual teams are playing a much larger role in the economics of business.

Having a virtual workforce, however, also creates many business benefits for the organization that cannot be ignored. The virtual worker gets freedom and flexibility not only over where they live but how and the organization gets to hire valuable talent wherever that talent resides. The ability to hire regardless of location, an expanded talent pool, lower real estate costs, a reduction in business and travel expenses and happier and more productive workers are only a few of the benefits. Workers have a more flexible lifestyle and spend more time with their families. It saves everybody money and provides opportunities for people who may otherwise not be able to be a part of the workforce. The virtual workplace creates value to the environment as well. It cuts down on gasoline consumption and decreases smog and pollution. But the true value comes from what the virtual worker can contribute both in terms of knowledge and performance.

When power and performance are not part of the same structure this can create problems within the organization. A significant amount of research has been conducted in the last decade, and most of it suggests that organizations are reluctant to give up the hierarchy. Virtual teams are good at circumventing structure to facilitate speed and availability. Organizational structure can vanish while accomplishing project objectives and goals but the hierarchy remains. The hierarchy operates outside of the world of the virtual environment. In many cases it is still alive and well in the C Suite at corporate headquarters.

Very little research exists on what happens to power when the organization is horizontal. What has happened to this point is that organizations have relied on the past. We have tried to apply theories of management and leadership that are centuries old to the virtual environment (Hornett, 2004). Organizations do not want to give up the power structure. This makes it very difficult to manage the invisible. There is a lot more invisible in the lack of support for virtual workers than the fact they are just working off site.

Virtual workers struggle with invisibility. They are concerned that what they do is not seen or recognized by the organization's leadership. Does management know how hard I'm working? How do I know what is really going on because no one tells me anything? They often feel like they are out of sight, out of mind and out of touch. Virtual workers also struggle with finding their "off" button. A common complaint is "I feel like I am always on. I am always working." They lack boundaries, both personal and professional, and often feel like they are being exploited. But more importantly they don't feel like they are part of the club. Organizations are currently not very likely to support virtual workers in a way that strengthens them as individuals or as productive performers within the organization.

Value is created in the virtual workplace by offering both flexibility and strong support. Employees need to be given the freedom and the power to run their own show, to create the balance between their work commitments and their personal lives. Management needs to communicate clearly the business objectives that must be met and provide the road map to get there. Expectations need to be more clearly defined, check-ins more frequent, and collaboration more regular. This lowers risk of stress on the individual. It allows fear to dissolve and creativity and innovation to flourish.

True value is developed through encouraging and supporting innovation and creativity. Creativity and innovation are only fostered when the mission is transparent and the communication and expectations are clear. Creativity has a much better chance of thriving in a diverse and global environment. The organization wants to support this talent by developing the skills that give virtual workers the resources to explore a global range of challenges and perspectives.

Working virtually means both the worker and the organization need to develop a different set of core skills. Working in the virtual environment means greater freedom, and with greater freedom comes more responsibility. The ability to act with autonomy and self-manage is only one part of the skill set. Workers also need to be able to set and enact priorities, be authentically productive, make responsible choices and align connections (Baggio, 2014). Virtual workers need the confidence and self-reliance to overcome obstacles, the self-discipline and personal project management skills to get work done on time and contribute their expertise. But the organization needs to get involved in this process also.

Organizations need to encourage this type of behavior, to allow the employee to take ownership of their work, their schedule and their performance. They need to empower the employee and encourage them to succeed. They need to support engagement and productivity through clearly communicated expectations, well defined performance goals and mutually agreed upon objectives. And then, most importantly, they need to let the employee go. The biggest challenge to success in the virtual environment is leadership. Leading virtually means leading differently. Leaders in the virtual workplace should listen between the lines and communicate clearly and intuitively. They need to have and to communicate clear expectations for performance, accountability and measurement.

Goals, deadlines and accountabilities create the roadmap for success. These need to be defined, communicated and reinforced. Leadership will also want to be transparent. Deceitful practices and hidden agendas do not do well in the virtual environment. This is an environment where trust is paramount and lack of trust can sabotage even the best of intentions. Trust is difficult to gain and easy to lose. No virtual workplace can succeed without trust in strong leaders.

Leaders in the virtual workplace need enhanced capabilities to manage independent and autonomous individuals. The old methods do not work. They need advanced communication skills, intuitive listening skills, trust building, and inspirational skills, and above all strong project management and accountability. They need to be able to deal with ambiguity and change and to reach and connect in a way that supports both the virtual worker and the business's objectives. The virtual leader needs to be focused on and deliver results. Value in the virtual workplace is all about delivering the goods. This ability comes by aligning connections. It is the job of virtual leadership to set up enough touchpoints and the right touchpoints to get this done.

Touchpoints   The virtual world is all about connections and connecting. Leaders in the virtual environment need to be effective communicators. They need to build relationships in an environment that is fast paced, remote and where distractions abound. To build a relationship, you have to touch someone. Not necessarily physically but certainly emotionally and cognitively. Relationships are built on touchpoints. Touchpoint is a term used to describe the interface between two things. Companies interface with customers and employees though many different channels: distribution, communication, service, public relations, investor relations and human resources. Virtual leadership is about creating and supporting touchpoints. Touchpoint leadership is a multi-dimensional strategic approach that focuses on optimizing performance.

Touchpoint leadership creates relationships that support the whole person and meet the business's objectives. This is customarily done through roles. In relationships, people play roles. This is how they connect. For example, in a marriage someone is a "husband" and someone is a "wife." In a friendship, both parties are "friends." In relationships, these roles often come with preconceived meaning. Developing meaning that works for both sides is one of the big challenges to leading in the virtual world. One of the biggest obstacles of leading a virtual workforce successfully is a traditional management mindset. Notice that roles are nouns. In the virtual work environment, we are interested in verbs. Performance and results are achieved with verbs.

Creating touchpoints in the virtual work environment is not always easy or automatic. The economics of virtual work, however, makes it an undertaking that can bring very positive bottom line results for the business and the individual. The first step is to get honest, and take stock of where you are and where you want to be. Leaders are often in denial about fear, loss of control, the "I can't see them I can't manage them" mentality. What more commonly surfaces is a distorted rational that claims "We need to be together to bond, collaborate, and create," which is just an excuse for "I don't trust them. If I am not watching them, they are not working, and I don't know how to control that or motivate these people!"

Touchpoints come in many different sizes and shapes. There are three general categories or types of touchpoints required to lead, inspire and measure virtual workplace performance: conceptual, transactional, and actual. Each of these general categories can be broken down into other categories. What is important is not the labels. What is critical is that the organization realizes that it touches the virtual worker in many ways, some invisible, some prescribed and some real.

Conceptual touchpoints include the organizational culture, shared perceptions, and views. Conceptual touchpoints can include many different channels from branding to social media to any number of internal and external influences. Conceptual touchpoints include the semantics of the organization and the intangible influences that can affect human behaviors. This includes how the organization knows itself, expresses itself and identifies the fundamental things that make it what it is. It can include the little things some individuals deal with day to day. There are internal and external conceptual touchpoints. Conceptual touchpoints are invisible and intangible but still influence the performance of the individual. Often, we attribute these to the organizational culture and the economic climate.

Transactional touchpoints are operational interfaces that impact how work gets done. These are the organizational charts, procedure manuals, business processes, operational diagrams, performance requirements or anything else that seeks to capture relationships of importance within the organization. This can be the basis for the actual touchpoints but the two should not be confused. Often, they are not the same. Transactional touchpoints include the organization's business strategy, the political structures and the information systems. Transactional touchpoints include procedures and frameworks. Companies develop these in many ways. Frequently they are distinct to the organization, people, and market. These touchpoints are often entrenched in history and seldom examined.

Actual touchpoints are the interfaces that really happen. These are the interactions between leaders and workers, workers and workers, worker and the organizational infrastructure, and workers and their performance tasks. These are the real interactions. Vicarious touchpoints are actual touchpoints that are observed from a distance. Actual touchpoints are the procedures and processes we really experience, both the good and not so good.

Touchpoints affect the emotional, mental and physical wellbeing of the virtual worker. They can be very supportive and provide reassurance or very disruptive and contribute to stress and anxiety. There can be too many or not enough touchpoints. They can be restrictive or supportive and imagined or real. The challenge is to establish touchpoints that both support the virtual worker and meet the business objects. Although flexibility, responsiveness and connections are important, what really matters in the virtual workplace is results (Rea & Field, 2012).

Listening Between the Lines

Organizations and other individuals touch us in many ways. Organizations are essentially networks of people who are joined together through interactions and form relationships. Communicating expectations, goals, objectives, deadlines, knowledge, support and efficacy cements relationships. A wide range of work environments may be considered to be virtual: global work teams, geographically dispersed project teams, inter-organizational groups, non-traditional work places (hotels, home or work centers) and non-traditional roles (micro workers, experts or consultants). Team structures and communication procedures unite or separate people in the virtual environment. Effective leaders not only know how to navigate within the structures and procedures, they know how to read between the lines (Watson-Manheim & Belanger, 2002).

At the heart of performance is communication-based work practices. These practices can be accomplished by conversations. In the virtual world, how those practices take place depends not only on the individuals involved but on the technology used and the affordances of that technology. The virtual environment is complex and the modes for communication areas exploding. In the virtual environment multiplicity is the norm. It is normal for virtual worker to use a multitude of different technologies and work at a variety of locations.

It is also typical to work with a wide variety of colleagues from many different areas. The virtual worker usually works on an assortment of teams and assumes many different roles simultaneously. They may belong to several task forces, work on several project teams, and belong to a department or division or a work group. What develops is multiple relationships. Managing multiple relationships can be challenging. If we can eliminate the obvious, and assume that communicating via all these different technologies is not the same as being in a F2F meeting, then the question becomes: What do we need to do to use these technologies effectively and support virtual workers and the organization?

Relationships and emotional connections in a world geographically distributed are extremely important. Many organizations have a huge challenge with onboarding for this reason. It is important to know who to call when you need something and then how to read the person when they respond. Many people find it difficult to be effective until they know the right people and establish the right relationships. Relationship development is clearly a pathway to success. Collecting information and sharing knowledge effects performance success. (Watson-Manheim & Belanger, 2002).

Many managers and supervisors in the virtual environment need to learn new communication skills and intuitive listening. The level and effectiveness of this type of listening impacts information overload and establishes trust and reliance. Creating personal relationships and developing trust when there are limited facial expressions, physical cues and body language requires creating new and different touchpoints. This usually means more communication and touching base more frequent-ly. Regular updates and status reports will help, but intuitive listening is about more than formal communication channels. It is the ability to read people eyes, their faces, their expressions on video chats and their tone of voice in emails. This allows us to touch the other person at just the right time and in just the right way. Communicating in the virtual environment requires unconventional thinking and a willingness to take a few calculated risks (Rea & Field, 2012).

What we say and what we mean are not always the same. Human beings are complex social animals. They have an inherent desire to know what their territory looks like and how to find their place in it. Often this is done with messages that fly below the radar. Reading these messages takes discipline and a well–tuned willingness to connect with the individual. This is a very different mindset than an approach that struggles to maintain control over people, projects, and deadlines. Many managers believe that virtual collaboration can undermine authority. Trust or lack of trust is what happens when we fear we are losing control when we can't see what is going on. One of the biggest challenges in leading in the virtual workplace is the change in mindset. Managers are no longer managing people's time and activities. They are accountable for results. Being responsible for results require leaders to step up and take ownership.

Case in Point: Silver, Halpern and Roselle, LLC

Silver, Halpern and Roselle, LLC is a national accounting firm whose main business is in three areas: Accounting, Tax and Audit. Their reputation is excellent and is based on great service and trust. Their customers respect them, trust their advice and stay with them for a long time. This reputation is achieved by state of the art computer systems, analytical databases and a variety of tools the managers and accountants use when consulting with the clients. Most of these programs are custom to Silver, Halpern and Roselle.

The firm hires expert technical people to develop and maintain the custom applications that support the business. The software applications integrate tax laws and the coding is extremely technical. It requires attention to detail and a high level of skill. The people who write these custom computer applications must be proficient in both tax law and programming skills. New tax laws are always being applied for the United States and foreign countries. These changes must be integrated into the existing systems quickly and flawlessly or the fallout could be very detrimental.

There are four programmers that work as subcontractors for Silver, Halpern and Roselle. They live in New York, Boston and Philadelphia. Everyone is on the East Coast of the United States. They only get together twice a year at the Silver, Halpern and Roselle holiday party and at the summer company picnic. They are connected to each other via email, a synchronous/video-chat platform and telephone. Formal meetings are rare but it is not at all unusual for informal meetings to occur among the programing staff.

Meet the Staff   George Anderson is a tax lawyer, a graduate of University of Massachusetts and a former hockey player. He is married with three young children and has a wife who works full time in downtown Boston. He is the stay-at-home Dad and 35 years old. George has been working for Silver, Halpern and Roselle for eight years and is the oldest and longest standing member of the programming group. He is responsible for all system analytics and design changes. George also functions as the trainer and onboarding specialist. He is the main contact point for the group and is the "team leader" and ultimately responsible for projects being on time and meeting the budget. He is also busy with soccer games, coaching baseball, dance lessons and basic household duties. He lives in a suburban area of Boston.

Carol Creig is a tax accountant and computer science double major from Boston College. She is 32 years old and has been with the group for two years. She is single and lives on a farm in New Hampshire and loves hunting and fishing. Carol is a full time partner and rarely comes into the city.

Margaret Harrison is a tax lawyer and a Wharton MBA. She lives in the Chestnut Hill area of Philadelphia and is 39 years old. Currently single, she likes to golf and play tennis and travel. She has been with the team four years and enjoys her autonomy. She works out of her apartment.

Jim Morrelli is a programmer and lives in New York. His wife is a corporate attorney and they have four children ages twelve, six, four and two. They have an apartment in the city and all the children go to public schools. Jim is interested in his job but he is also a base guitarist and plays in a band.

The main way this team communicates is via email. They send many emails back and forth every day. They can call or text each other anytime. They meet on Monday morning by video chat and have a rule that when you are online you have the chat stream open. They are all hourly employees except for George who was made a salaried employee last year. They have an agreement that they can work wherever and whenever they way want as long as the work gets done on time. Flexibility is important to all of them and their lifestyles. They enjoy their freedom and none of them plans on ever working in an office full time again.

Jim is a classic programmer and loves to create code that helps him to update these systems more quickly. On a recent project, he created a "shortcut" that allowed them to get the job done in much less time than it usually takes. The problem came in when they realized that this was cutting into Carol, Margaret and especially Jim's wages, because all three are paid by the hour. Rather than tell George about the shortcut, they kept it from him because they feared he would tell his boss and then they would make less money. They could have more personal time if they met the deadlines and used the shortcut. This all worked well for a while.

In a casual conversation Margaret was having with a friend over lunch who knows several people who work at the firm, she leaked that they had an innovation that was giving them a great deal of time and that they now had more free time for their own interests. Margaret talked to her friend and her friend talked to Art Silver. Art is George's boss. Art became very concerned because no one had mentioned this to him. He wondered what the shortcut was and why the billable hours had not changed. He contacted George. George assured him that he knew nothing about this, but rather than this making Art feel better, he became more concerned. If George didn't know this was going on, what else didn't he know? Art decided to call everyone back into the office, Jim and Margaret informed the company that they were not about to move.

It looks like virtual work might be coming to an end at Silver, Halpern and Roselle.

1. What steps would you take to assure the best interests of the firm?

2. What is fundamentally wrong with this situation? What steps need to be taken to fix it?

3. How is the virtual nature of the work environment playing into the decisions being made?

4. What impact does technology have and what other technology might be used?

5. What steps would you take to change this situation for the better? Is it salvageable? Would you fire anyone?

6. Are their ethical issues here?

7. If you were discussing touchpoints, what would they look like? How might that have impacted the situation? How would you change those going forward?

Exercise 1: Create a Touchpoint Analysis Grid

Day/Date Name	Monday	Tuesday	Wednesday	Thursday	Friday	Saturday

Managing in the virtual environment is very different than managing F2F. Like so many other things where technology is the interface, it can even be counterintuitive. There is no doubt that the trend toward a growing virtual workforce will continue. Organization leaders need to learn how to effectively manage in the virtual workplace and this presents a challenge. A survey conducted by Cisco in 2006 determined that 37% of the managers surveyed found managing virtual teams to be a very different experience. It takes more time to produce a connected level of engagement. It requires a very different style of management. Core competencies for managing virtually include a strong affinity toward technology and good social skills. Psychological profiles of managers that were successful included resilience, low levels of neuroticism, extroversion, self-confidence and effective communication (Sundin, 2010).

Communication in any organization is a complex process. In a F2F environment it can be challenging. We communicate primarily to get what we want. We all do. We come at communication from our own perspective and we approach it with our own limitations. We want positive tangible results from our efforts both physically and emotionally. We want to be understood, to get our point across. If the other person seems to be okay with it, all the better. But for most of us understanding is secondary to being understood. We all think communicating is easy. We talk to others all day long. We can be in the same room or halfway across the planet because we have multiple devices that can connect us in an instant. We operate as if what we mean is what we say and what we say is what they hear, what we put out is exactly what they take in. Well, not exactly! Actually, it is miracle we can communicate at all. There are distractions all around us.

Chapter 2

Achieving Effective Virtual Communication

**The single biggest problem in communication is the illusion it has taken place.
—George Bernard Shaw**

Effective Virtual Communication

35

We all have patterns of communication. Some of these patterns we learned in childhood. Some we have picked up from interacting with other humans along the way. In the F2F environment, we have a background structure to ground this communication. We put on our business voice for the office. We use kiddy talk to communicate with the little ones and pets at home. And we have nonverbal gestures. We raise an eyebrow, roll our eyes, tilt our head, or wrinkle our forehead to show what we really mean. In the virtual environment, these cues are filtered. The nonverbal cues are gone or at least not as strong as they are in a physical environment. This leads to more misinterpretation. When we are paying attention, our ability to interpret communication is the strongest. Most of us are limited in that. Our attention wanders.

Because we are human beings, we are easily distracted. Focusing our attention is something that is up to each individual. Our mental focus varies based on the amount and number of distractions available in our environment and our mind. Once we get focused, the interpretation of the input is up to each one of us. It is subjective. Each of us has a different perception of whatever is coming to us from our senses. Our interpretation and others' interpretation are different. Osmo Wiio, a famous Finnish communication scholar, developed what has affectionately come to be known as "Murphy's 7 Laws of Communication" or "Wiio's 7 Laws of Communication Failure." The central Wiio's law states that "communication usually fails, except by accident" (Hammock, 2013).

Each one of us has a narrative we go over in our minds that describes who and what we are. It is how we see ourselves and how we measure our worth. We each have unique personalities, self-concepts and self-efficacy. We compare ourselves to others, the media images we see. We review the roles we are expected to play and we develop a set of expectation about others and ourselves. When people and events match this set of expectations, we are usually happy or at least not unhappy. When things don't meet this set of expectations, we have a whole set of defensive tactics we use to defend our egos.

Psychologists have been studying the ways we defend our sense of self since (if not before) Freud. We evaluate our interactions and develop defenses when they do not meet our internal expectations. These expectations are developed over time from family relationships, social and cultural norms, and personal preferences. Our internal emotions quite often activate our external behaviors.

When we feel threatened, let down or otherwise negatively impacted by an event, a relationship or a circumstance, we use common forms of defense. Sometimes we avoid, deny or rationalize. Other times, we may intellectualize or project. Depending on our defensive approach, we will commonly respond in one of three voices: the child, the parent or the adult. The child is the natural, joyful creative, funny or angry voice that obeys. The parental voice is the one that scolds, orders, and tries to control or command. The adult voice, which is the one we want to use in business communication, is data-oriented and focused on problem solving. The adult voice is clear and wants to know the facts, not just be right. The adult wants to know all the information so that it can make an impartial and informed decision.

Most of us believe that what we think is true. Turns out that it is really just what we think. It is very difficult for humans to separate the thought and the thing. Our thoughts are really just that, our thoughts. Communication research supports the fact that the thought and the thing are often not the same. We have a natural tendency to have a bias toward ourselves! Often termed the self-serving bias or the vain brain, we defend our thoughts because they serve our positions. We communicate mostly to influence and persuade. When things don't go our way, we find a way to justify that by judging, devaluing and trying to control. We are always trying to understand what is going on and how that impacts us.

Every environment has a certain amount of "noise" in it. The virtual environment has more "noise" because the communication is being filtered through technology. There is the physical noise in the environment and the psychological noise in each party involved in the communication. It turns out that the psychological noise can be louder than most physical noise because this noise is created by emotions. It is not easy for us to get our meaning across. There can be big many differences between what we mean to say and how that communication is interpreted by the other person.

First, we are all different people with different backgrounds, different thought processes, different cultures, social economic groups, ethnicities, genders, religions, etc. We are different from one another in many ways. We are all unique individuals. We have different points of view and different agendas to accomplish. Sometimes this can all come together very easily and sometimes because of these differences we disagree. Disagreements can lead to disorder.

When we are trying to communicate with another individual it is important to identify what emotions we are bring to the conversation. It helps to identify those feelings. Put a reason behind why we are feeling what we are feeling. Anchor ourselves in the present. Most of us have a difficult time getting in touch with our own emotions let alone having empathy for someone else. Being able to communicate effectively in a virtual environment with others starts with knowing and owning yourself.

My earlier book, *The Pajama Effect,* identified one of the biggest challenges of working in a virtual environment is that we are alone with ourselves. We can be our own best friend or worst enemy. It is almost entirely up to us. This is why learning to act with autonomy is so very important. Learning to slow those voices in our head down so that we can get a handle on what we are really saying to ourselves and what we are saying about others is imperative. We are programed to focus on the negatives in others. This goes back to the dinosaurs and has to do with the development of the brain and the survival instinct. It served us well then but it does not serve us well now.

We also have a tendency, because of the wiring in our brain's circuitry, to believe what we have always believed, and think what we have always thought. Therefore, we run the same videos over and over in our heads and ruminate monologues again and again and again. It has to do with our neuro circuitry. This causes quick reactions. When we communicate virtually we need to take extra care that we are not reacting.

Technology disconnects us and distracts us. It removes us from the here and now. It is easier to detach and not really listen in the virtual environment because to an extent we are already detached. However, if we are not paying attention we can tune out and start to critically judge people, especially before we have heard their point of view. We overgeneralize, awfulize and engage in fortune telling. We categorize, pass judgment and label. In order to get to the adult voice, we want to describe the facts. Like Sargent Friday said, "Nothing but the facts, Mam!" It helps to identify and describe our emotions. This can help us think it through to the end. Will what we are about to communicate give us the results we want? Do we have all the facts?

We want to remain open to new information and focus on outcomes. Appreciation and respect for the position of others will change the way we communicate. We want to focus our conversation on what is working, not what isn't. We want to align our conversations so that they add value to the outcome we seek, not detract from it. And we want to always ask the other party for input. How do they see the situation? What is their point of view? What do they have to offer as a solution? Keep the conversation open so that we don't close it down. Be supportive, appreciative and understanding.

When we are connected via technology, nothing is what it seems to be. We don't want to be definite but rather stay conditional. We need to use phrases like "under these circumstances," or "it seems to me" this is what happened. This goes a long way toward establishing equality and softening authoritative or demanding communication styles. "It's not what you say but how you say it" is true in the virtual world, too! Don't be afraid to establish connections using small talk in the virtual world. Just because it is business and just because we are connected digitally doesn't mean we don't have to connect personally.

Small talk goes a long way in establishing connections. Simple kindness statements and connection like "How are you? How's it going? What's up? How are you doing?" are natural and automatic in the F2F world. We need to consciously establish these same kinds of connections in the virtual environment. Chapter 5 will discuss this in depth. All communication in the virtual environment is "me to you" (M2Y) communication. This social and enjoyable chit chat is important because it connects us to others in a positive and playful way. It establishes a tone and sets the stage for a relaxed and sociable connection. We remember these kinds of emotional tones. There is research that suggests that we need five positive statements to balance out every negative one.

Often as leaders we are put in the situation that we want to exercise some control in the meeting or online conversation. We think the way to do this is to use a controlling tone and language in the conversation. We set the agenda and diligently go over the items on it. If someone doesn't agree or is out of sorts, we are pretty sure that if we are convincing enough we will influence them to change to our way of seeing things. Based on our information, it is obvious that they need to see thing our way! If we just stick to our guns, they will change. And if they don't there must be something wrong with them. There must be a personal issue that is causing them to resist our point of view. This is very thin ice. It can lead to more demanding language and arguments.

This can also be a power play. People working in a virtual environment can be especially vulnerable because (or maybe as the management) you can feel vulnerable and ineffective. They feel like they can't control what they can't see. They think if they could just have us back in the office where they could observe us then they could determine if we were really working hard. If we were dedicated, we would be there early and leave late. But in the virtual world this doesn't work. The real dynamic here is that they never really had control of us. Unless they are comfortable in their role, their power and their responsibilities, they can feel very vulnerable. Not being F2F can cause us to feel vulnerable. When people feel vulnerable, they can feel threatened.

There is a big difference between visibility in an organization and transparency. Visibility is putting everything out there and can add to the noise. Transparency is a focus on clarity, openness and unambiguity. This duality can be fueled by change and exemplified in the virtual environment. In the virtual world it is easier to have disagreements. This means if our communication is going to be effective it must be intentionally relevant, truthful and clear. Visibility can still present false information. Transparency allows everyone to see what is being presented. It is a 360-degree view that supports total and complete clarity.

Our Emotion How we communicate in the virtual world can have a huge impact on our success, particularly if our mission is to persuade, which is often the case for leaders, teachers, trainers, sales people and managers. Part of learning to communicate effectively in a virtual environment is training ourselves to really care about the other person. We are sometimes too interested in delivering our message and not willing to really hear the other point of view. We give little or no acknowledgment for their side of the story before we proceed to tell them ours. Our first approach is usually to reason with them. If that doesn't work, we go on the attack. We turn to attack talk because we are frustrated.

In a F2F environment people are not always easy to deal with. They come in many different varieties. When getting what we want is threatened we become defensive. Some of us are aggressive, some passive and some passive aggressive. We all use some of these tactics some of the time. When a rational approach isn't working to get our needs met, we revert to an emotional one.

We get especially frustrated when an issue has been going on for a while. If we have tried before to make progress and don't seem to be making progress this contributes to even more frustration. A persistent problem increases our resistance. This can often lead to even more attempts on our part to control the conversation. We attempt to play hard ball when our more rational and positive tactics have not gotten us the results we wanted. We put ourselves in a position of competing for control. We often resort to the fight or flight response. Many of these approaches originate in our subconscious but most importantly they can make people feel badly and they hardly ever work. Often these are emotional attacks and usually they are negative. Depending on how desperate we are, we may resort to name calling or labeling, villainizing or demoralizing: "You are an idiot."

Emotions are a part of who and what we are as human beings. We learn to use them from the time we are babies to get our needs met. When we are unhappy, we cry. When we are really unhappy, we cry louder. As we grow from children into adults, we either learn to manage our emotions or our emotions manage us. We learn early on that we can sometimes get our own way by walking away from the conversation, slamming our fists and leaving. It takes practice not to revert to that childlike reaction when our needs are not being met. Many of us have a reactive need to be right. Sometimes that need is so strong that it keeps us from addressing the problem. The question becomes: "Do you want to be right or do you want to solve the problem?" In order to decide, we make inferences. Inferences in the F2F world are often based on observation. In the virtual world, we make inferences based more on instinct. We select data from the past more than from observable behaviors. We draw conclusions and form ideas from our own inner voices and what these voices tell us. To do this, however, we have to slow down and sort out our point of view from theirs. Often, we become automatically convinced that our point of view is the only point of view. Our beliefs are reality. When our beliefs are our perception of reality avoiding the conversation will not solve the problem. As Harvey Cox said, "Not to decide is to decide." In the virtual environment, not having the courage to have the conversations, the critical conversations, will deepen the divide. This will further damage the relationship. The lack of visual cues already makes it difficult to read intention and interpret meaning. Silence in this environment can be devastating. To solve problems, we want to engage in a dialogue. This means we need to get both parties talking. Dialogue, by definition, is between two parties. To have a dialogue, we must suspend the notion that one party is right and the other party is wrong. We should stop pointing fingers and openly engage in a conversation.

The best way to get a conversation started is to do it ourselves. Don't wait for the other person to create the conversation. Open the conversation in a non-accusatory way and use I statements rather than you statements. You statements carry with them a feeling of judgment and blame. We want to state in terms of "who, what, when, where and why by using a calm voice and "I." For example: "I would prefer if the committee would...," "Given my choice, I would rather the customer would...," "I choose to believe that...," etc." We want to describe our position and not point fingers or pass judgment. Nothing will cause disengagement to accelerate more quickly than asserting blame and shame.

The biggest challenge in this type of communication, for most people, is to slow down long enough to do it. Using the first person has the effect of cutting down on critical judgment. This opens the communication by taking away the blame. Whether we agree or disagree, it normalizes the situation. Try to avoid statements like "I think you are...," which is just a way of hiding the "you are" part of the communication and is still a judgment. Use present tense as much as possible. Avoid the future and the past tenses. Also avoid should have, would have and could have statements as much as possible.

In a F2F environment, we use the body to request attention. We lean in, lean out and nod our heads. We use a smile to engage and a tilt of the head to acknowledge. In the virtual world, even with video, you lose a lot of these cues. It is important to take advantage of the cues we do have and maybe even overemphasize them a little. Active listening, which will be discussed in Chapter 4, is a way of communicating. Mindful engagement lets the other party know that we are paying attention and that they are important. It acknowledges that they have something to say and that we are there to listen. This takes conscious effort on our part. Most of us have less than stellar listening skills. Our brains are quick and our focus is scattered. Making it even more challenging, we have these things called emotions that keep hijacking our conscious efforts. Many of us have issues with emotional self-management. We are hard wired to react. We think really fast. This is not the best combination for trust (Bollow, 2010).

Facial expressions serve as a window to the emotions. They are one way we pick up on nonverbal cues. Researchers have studied facial expressions for the last 50 years, some claiming that facial expressions are a way of determining our internal mental state. Recently there has been a surge of work on facial recognition using computer algorithms to identify characteristics and emotional states. Often there is a distinction made between those emotions that are actively created for strategic goals or deliberate and those that are uncontrollable reactions and automatic. Either way, facial expressions are one way that virtual interfaces allow us to effectively transmit emotions.

The more we move toward the Internet of Things (IOT), the more we will learn about user interface systems and the impact of emotions. Some research already shows that matching a car's warning voice to the mood of the driver (cheerful or sad) decreases accident rates as compared to a mismatch. The lesson here is matched moods can enhance efficiency and productivity (Bailenson et al., 2007). Understanding and interpreting where the other person is really coming from is an intuitive listening skill that is developed by successful virtual mangers.

Virtual managers need to provide direction and remove all (or at least most) ambiguity. Managing virtual workers is a highly centralized and structured function. Virtual teams function best with formalized roles and responsibilities including those of the management. Virtual communication requires a broader base of skills. These skills can vary based on the distance and diversity of the workers. Decision making is often rooted in the culture we come from and different cultures have different approaches. Virtual teams need a very detailed explanation of how decisions will be made. Management needs to be aware of cultural differences and be open to trying new approaches (Evans, 2011), which is just the opposite of what the business schools have been teaching about leadership and loosely defined job descriptions and sharing roles. This is partly because the decisions in a virtual workplace are arrived at differently.

Along with being highly self-motivated, virtual managers need to be organized and capable of building relationships. Short but frequent contacts are essential for keeping remote workers engaged, informed and interested in the daily happenings. These short connections can help to keep workers interested and relationships strong. Virtual managers need the ability to acknowledge contributions and provide informal feedback. Everyone likes to feel important and that includes virtual workers. Managing performance is most effective in the virtual environment when management and the worker together establish how performance will be assessed and evaluated.

Trust is Everything

Virtual workers are most productive when they self-manage. Trust is what allows them to thrive. This includes acting with autonomy and setting and enacting their own priorities. Many organizations find this the most difficult part of having a virtual workplace. Some have even reverted to using software and video-enhanced monitoring techniques but research strongly supports that this kind of attempt at control backfires. Looking over the shoulder of remote employees can have a very detrimental effect on motivation and productivity (Sundin, 2010). In the virtual workplace, trust is measured almost entirely in terms of reliability.

There are three major factor affecting trust in virtual workplace environments: the trust team members have in each other, the trust they have in leadership, and the trust they have in the technology. Trusting in each other to do the job and share knowledge is at the core of a company's success. This is why so many organizations will have annual or biannual F2F meetings. Once we meet F2F, we tend to build more trusting relationships. It is important for individuals to be given the time and support to build strong relationships. Leaders play a huge role in facilitating this relationship connection. Leaders are responsible, together with the workers, for establishing the roles each party will play in collecting, synthesizing and distributing the knowledge. Knowledge is the currency of trust in a virtual environment. Knowledge is power. The organizational culture wants to support trust and allow employees to make independent and autonomous decisions (Ferrell & Herb, 2012). In turn, virtual employees need to be reliable and trustworthy enough to get the job done.

We can create team agreements or contracts if we want, but it is not always necessary or effective. It is helpful if we establish communication norms upfront. For example, establishing parameters on how and when we will schedule meetings, how we will handle time zone differences, and what the roles and responsibilities for team members are can clarify expectations. Clear expectations are important for trust.

Virtual employees also need to reasonably trust the technology to work. Whatever we are using for regular communication needs to work as seamlessly and transparently as possible. It is important that everyone trusts the technology. Establishing some ground rules can be very helpful too. What do we use and when (email, chat, intranet, phone, videoconference), and what is the expected response time? What criteria do we agree to for prioritizing issues? What are the rules for virtual meetings? Clear ground rules and expectations can avert burnout (Evans, 2011).

There are many different methods leadership can use to establish these guidelines. Leadership can determine the plan for meetings by defining simple and regular meeting outcomes. They can set the agenda by determining what key decisions need to be achieved and send a list of attendees. Some organizations will create charters or contracts on how interactions will take place. They will specify formal goals and policies and formalize the communication channels and limits. Others will try to achieve this by collaboration and consensus building. Whichever method you use, it is important is that boundaries are defined and clearly communicated (Ferrell & Herb, 2012). Simple performance indicators, when communicated, can go a long way in supporting better virtual interactions.

Video has made virtual communication much better. Effectively communicating, however, usually means writing expectations down and distributing them ahead of time. This allows people to plan their responses and questions. When we have the opportunity use video conferencing, remember the fewer the people the better. One to one works much better than one to many in the virtual environment. When you end a communication session, wrap it up with an action plan that is clear and concise. Let the participating parties know exactly what is expected. This helps to build trust.

Burnout can be a problem in the virtual workplace. Extreme absenteeism, substance abuse and stress related health problems can all be a result of burnout. Burnout is what happens when humans do not have boundaries and companies expect people to be "on" 24/7/365. Virtual workers can feel very isolated, and unclear expectations can add to this stress. Virtual workers can feel invisible. Some virtual workers complain that their work is less appreciated. Burnout can be avoided and many of these difficulties subverted with strong management and a solidly executed communication approach. Regular communication and networking will allow a manager to create a supportive environment that replicates the informal professional development processes the traditional company environment provides. This can provide a sense of belonging and security, and it can ease the stress often associated with virtual worker burnout.

No doubt, the virtual workplace in its many forms will continue to grow. The millennial generation, now the largest part of the workforce, is demanding it. Our understanding of human interactions will continue to evolve and support this. Currently, we have both synchronous and asynchronous communication. Social presence plays a large role in either kind of connectivity. Social presence theory has been around for decades and is based on sharing emotions and personal interactions. Other connection models, like social information theory, suggest that if enough information is shared, strong relationships will develop (Warkentin,1999).

Regardless of the theory, achieving effective communication in virtual environments requires effort and affective connection. In most cases it also requires a well-constructed and executed plan on the part of the management. Consideration needs to be given to achieving the business goals and supporting the virtual worker's production and their general overall well-being. Leaders can translate these efforts to lower turnover and, most importantly, happier and more well-adjusted virtual workers.

Effective communication in any environment can be challenging. Achieving virtual communication that works well takes effort. It is important to establish a sense of belonging and convey a sense of well-being and support. It takes effort to find ways to express in a virtual environment what is expressed non-verbally in a F2F encounter. Communication, like relationships, grows over time. Taking short-cuts can lead to misunderstandings and ineffective interactions. Because technologies filters nonverbal messages, it is important to put extra effort into establishing human to human bonding. Cultural differences can play a big role in virtual communication but ultimately it boils down to trust. It is critical that trust is a two-way street (Sasti, 2013). It is not the quantity of communication that matters. It is the quality and predictability of communication that is the most critical. Remember in communicating virtually not to mistake noise for information or visibility for transparency.

Case in Point: Termer Construction Management, Inc.

Termer Construction provides project managers and onsite supervision for large industrial and commercial construction projects. This is a family-owned business that has been around for 75 years. Founded in the Pittsburgh area, they have branched out to four continents. The positions for Termer employees are long term. Some are hired locally and many relocate for the duration of the jobs. Everything about Termer is about managing time and money, including managing people. Recently, on a large job in Manhattan things have not been going smoothly.

It became clear that the crew needed to have a meeting. The home office reported several issues. They were falling behind on the project because clashes between Termer and several of the other companies were getting ugly. Even the communication within Termer was going downhill fast, with lots of resentment, infighting and dwelling on past conflicts. The main project manager is Joe Stevens. He works in the home office with his assistant, MaryAnn Zyleski. John Peters is the onsite project manager.

It was clear to Joe that John was more interested in being right than anything else. He had been given chances, coaching and advice. Joe was going to have to let him go. Here is the conversation between John and Joe:

To...	John.Peters@TremerCM.com
Cc...	
Subject	Sorry to have to do this

John: I think it is best if you do not come into the job tomorrow morning. I will let headquarters know that you no longer are on our payroll. I think after our "air out session" it is better if we part ways. Our HR people will be in touch with you by the end of the week. I am going to recommend we pay you through the end of the month. I think there has been too much water over the dam to turn back the clock. I wish you the best moving forward. Joe

Meet the Staff

Joe Stevens has been with the company for many years. In his late fifties, he had seen projects like this go south before because of people not pulling together. "They are spending way too much time gathering evidence about being right and not nearly enough time on the job. I know I probably started this but the gossip has gotten out of hand."

MaryAnn Zyleski was in her forties and single. She too has been around the company for a long time. "I think we need a no gossip policy and we need to enforce it. I am willing to have the difficult conversations with the subs, but I am not sure John is."

John Peters came from a local construction company and was not used to the pace or the rules that Termor adhered to. He did his best, but he was just lost.

Eventually Joe concluded this was not going to work out. Joe sent the email Sunday evening before he went to bed, at about 11:30PM.

Questions

1. Do you think handled this well? Does Termer Corporate need a policy about this issue? What might it say?

2. What does this tell you about Termer's ability to support virtual workers in the field? Did Joe use the right communication approach? Would a phone call have been better?

3. Why do you think he sent this email? Was he using the right tool, at the right time, for the right connection? Why do companies want to be very specific about tools and how they are used in the virtual environment?

4. Can MaryAnn really have that conversation with the subs?

5. What can Termer do to prevent this kind of situation from happening again?

Exercise 1:
Virtual
Communication

1. What are your employment policies concerning virtual connections and communication?

2. Do they cover text messaging, social media, email, and video chat? Anything else?

3. Do you have boundaries on usage? Where is it written down? Are workers aware of these policies? Are they easy to read and understand?

4. If there was one area of improvement that you as a leader would like to see, what would that be?

We are always "on" and always connected. We are connected by technology that knows where we are and can recommend what we do next. Over two-thirds of us report feeling totally overwhelmed. We rate everything. The judgment is public and constant. It gives us a sense of "control" in an environment that is overpowering. In a hyper-connected world, with emails and messages bombarding us day and night, with advertisements smart enough to be tailored to our "personas" and personal preferences, we feel the need to control, maybe more now than we ever did, because this nonstop work environment makes us feel so out of control. Improving productivity and the work experience are top priorities in the virtual workplace. Open feedback is trending, but like all change that breaks down the barriers between employees and leadership, it requires honest and new ways of thinking.

Beliefs that don't empower people disempower people. In the virtual workplace, it is easy to feel disconnected, disempowered and dismissed. There is a lot of conversation these days about empowerment, critical thinking skills and innovation, but few companies embrace these. These ideas are discomforting for management. By empowering people to think, do and act autonomously, we are relying on their ideas, thoughts and hearts to deliver the results. Most managers perceive innovation as a loss of control. It is much easier if people look like us, think like us and follow our ideas. After all, we have our beliefs and we believe them! Innovation and creativity are just the buzz words of the present moment. In time this too shall pass...or will it?

Autonomy gives people a chance to be who they are. Diversity and inclusion used to be lip service but

Chapter 3

Losing the Illusion of Control

**The closest to being in control we will ever be is in that moment that we realize we're not.
—Brian Kessler**

have grown into an integral part of the business plan. Why? Because it is profitable. Younger workers and older workers bring new and different ideas, experiences and ways of working. Some only want to work part time and others want flexible schedules. How to keep this diverse workforce focused and engaged is the topic of many business discussions. The definition of engagement, the work day, the project and the terms of employment are also evolving. We are more network-oriented and less physically attached. Companies like Uber, AirBnB and others have redefined "worker" and outsourcing. Almost 32% of the workforce is provisional. The sense of ownership has changed. It is time for our beliefs to change too (Bersin, 2016).

There is an insurance company in Cleveland that sent a small army of workers to a seminar to learn about managing workers in a virtual environment. The telecommuting policy was pretty simple: You can work from home two days a week as long as you live with in an 85-mile radius of corporate headquarters. Why 85 miles? It had something to do with "in case of an emergency." When asked why, the answer was "we want to keep control." Again, and again, I have heard that the number one reason people don't want to embrace the virtual workplace is they fear losing control.

Stereotyping, Depersonalizing and Controlling

Carl Jung and Sigmund Freud popularized the concept of an "unconscious mind," and ever since then people have been trying to figure it out. Terms like the unconscious, the subconscious and the implicit are used to describe a part of our mind. This is the part that carries around stereotypes, attitudes and biases that we act out and act upon but that we are not aware of with the conscious mind. These forces are involuntary and they are powerful. They influence our habits, perceptions, intentions and actions. Often, we base our decisions on these implicit influences. And we are not even aware they exist! The analogy often associated with Freud is that the conscious mind is equivalent to the "tip of an iceberg" and the unconscious mind, which is below the surface, is much larger and more powerful. Research attempting to map and measure how much is above the surface and how much is below the surface continues.

Over the last twenty years, neuroscience and psychology have generally accepted dual processing as the model for brain operations. Conscious thinking is deliberate, takes effort and is governed by logic and reason. Unconscious thinking (subconscious or implicit bias) is associative and relationship-based and is formed by observation and exposure. The key is that we are not necessarily aware of these concepts and they can be quite strong depending on how often, in what context and with what intensity they were formed. There are many excellent books on the subject including Daniel Kahneman's Thinking Fast and Slow (2011) and Charles Duhigg's The Power of Habit: Why We Do What We Do in Love and Business (2012). This under the surface part of our brain is influenced by media, upbringing, life experience and our environment. Everyone has it and everyone is influenced implicitly.

Changing unconscious bias is not easy. No one is ever completely free of unconscious bias. Psychology used to think that making people aware could make change easier but this has not been not substantiated by research. Awareness, though, is a first step. As Carl Jung stated, "until you make the unconscious conscious, it will direct your life and you will call it fate." What makes this even more interesting is that what we process unconsciously may not align with what we believe consciously. Society has come a long way in introducing us to diversity and inclusion. We have campaigned against stereotyping, depersonalizing and controlling bias but that has not eliminated them. Psychologist have been working to develop tests to measure unconscious associations but this is only so helpful (Kirwan, 2015).

As leaders in the virtual work environment, it is important to be mindful of what virtual workers are experiencing and help them become mindful of their actions and reactions so that they can respond rather than react. Keep in mind, the virtual culture within an organization and the F2F culture can be very different. Depending on how the organization is establishing touchpoints, virtual can be a very lonely and isolating experience. Understanding and addressing stereotyping, depersonalizing or controlling begins with understanding ourselves. Recognizing these in ourselves is a good place to start. Then we can begin to recognize them in others.

Stereotyping

Stereotyping is a group of beliefs held by one group of people about another group of people. There is a tendency to recognize but oversimplify with stereotypes. Stereotypes pigeonhole people into a group based on very limited information. When we stereotype we are not concerned about the person as an individual. We make people much more homogeneous than they are. We attribute general and similar characteristics to them, even if they don't apply. This creates differences and divisions between people where they may not be any. Negative stereotypes can severely limit communication in the virtual environment. These attitudes are severely damaging, especially when individuals try to communicate without traditional visual cues. In the virtual environment, the traditional cues to the emotions of the person are diffused and your own emotions are heightened. In a virtual environment, communication is me-to-you (M2Y) and much more personal.

Individuals are vastly different and come in many shapes and sizes. Stereotyping is a way of categorizing and labeling that dehumanizes. It discounts the vast array of human differences that make a person unique, distinct and an individual. It is human nature. A strong part of every language is labeling people, places and things. It is also human nature to have opinions and make judgments. But these labels bring along with them false expectations and predispositions. This can also create a backlash reaction where people react negatively when the people do not fit the stereotype. For example, we meet a woman who loves math and is superior with numbers there is something about her we just don't like. When we stereotype we judge by the expectations of others (Whelan, 2013). Stereotyping makes it very difficult to listen without prejudging the conversation. This is difficult in a F2F environment but even more difficult online. In order to lead in a virtual environment, we want to discover what stereotypes we hold on to and how this may influence our interactions.

Depersonalizing

Depersonalization is feeling detached from your own thoughts, feelings, emotions and behaviors. Depersonalization is divorcing or separating from the self. Any communication that is narrow and impersonal is even more so online. When we focus on projects and problems and forget that people are at the other end of the Gantt chart, it is all too easy to depersonalize. When we leave the everyday aspect of conversation out of the equation, it is easy to speak a monologue and not a dialogue. Chapter 5 is about M2Y (me to you) communication and FROG (family, recreation, occupation and goals), and explains the importance of establishing personal relationships. Collaboration online doesn't come from talking at but from consulting with the other person.

Many of our biases, evaluations and judgments are made because we depersonalize. Without eye contact or body language and other three-dimensional visual cues, it is much easier to depersonalize. These unconscious associations require less cognitive effort and become automatic and unconscious. These thought processes are difficult to recognize and override because they happen automatically and very quickly. Studies suggest that our brains process approximately 20,000,000 bits of information every second but our conscious minds handle only 40 or 50 of those bits.

Controlling   There is a deep unconscious bias towards controlling the worker in the workplace. The perception that workers are there to work less and management must keep them in line has a lot of history. Most of us have some implicit ideas about management. These implicit ideas can be difficult to deactivate because they can be pervasive and robust. Management is supposed to tell workers what to do, but telling doesn't sit well with the virtual environment. It goes against the ability of an individual to act with autonomy.

When we reduce the individual's sense of autonomy by limiting choices and decisions to predetermined constraints, we limit the individual's ability to respond. Any authoritarian style of communication can also increase negative feeling and resentments. When we feel that we are not in control, in a culture that is based on the idea that it is management's job to control outcomes, we are bound to feel negative. Then we begin to generate reasons to explain why this is accurate. The classic example is Yahoo's CEO Marrisa Mayer's 2013 "No Work from Home Memo." When something feels dangerous we create conscious and rational thoughts that justify our actions. Usually these decisions are emotional in nature. Our unconscious biases impact the way we perceive others and how we perceive ourselves. We make decisions that confirm what we already believe. This "conformational behavior" occurs unconsciously and in both positive and negative ways.

Collective unconscious organizational patterns enormously influence company culture and how an organization behaves. These patterns are deeply ingrained and it is very difficult for us to understand their impact. The collective unconscious is concealed from our conscious thinking. Nevertheless, it greatly impacts our decision making. We justify our decisions based on these buried beliefs. We think we are making these consciously but really the unconscious is running the show. These deeply seated beliefs are why it is so difficult to change organizational culture and why attempts to do so usually fail. Despite training and development efforts, the collective unconscious makes decisions, behaviors and choices using the same old patterns, values and norms because these are so deeply rooted. Nowhere is this truer than in the virtual workplace.

Flexible hours, working conditions and arrangements make logical sense. It allows people to meet personal and family needs, whether they are the needs of parents, children or personal. So companies have created policies in support of working virtually. Spoken or unspoken, written or not, the company will have a policy. However, when people take advantage of this opportunity and begin working virtually, they are considered less valuable, less dedicated and less promotable. The message is mixed and very confusing; the policy says it is okay but the culture says you are not a dedicated member of the team and therefore less valuable. This creates an undercurrent of stress and tension. Statistics confirm that the freedom to work virtually increases performance, increases employee satisfaction and reduces turnover. However, unconsciously people may believe differently and fear and mistrust prevail (Ross, 2008). Organizational cultures of fear and mistrust need to be replaced with cultures that support people working virtually. Clear, open and supportive communication and expectations can help to eliminate hidden issues of trust. After all, results are results.

Letting Go of a Culture of Control

Organizational culture is a hot topic. People all over in all types of organizations are talking about organizational culture. It is a mysterious term that describes the quality of an interaction-based environment. Although it is difficult to define, the assessment is usually all about "fit." If a person fits into the corporate culture, it just feels right. Culture can make employees feel like they belong and are more supported and recognized, or not. It affects our interactions with others, behaviors and processes. Culture can support our success or is a contributor to our unraveling. Virtual workers toggle between the organizational culture and the culture of their own personal environment. A personal environment that is quiet, focused and supportive will have a much different influence than one that is noisy, interrupted and negative.

Culture manifests itself through physical and nonphysical elements in the day to day workplace. It can contribute to our loyalty and enjoyment at work. In many ways, culture is a sum of the personalities and experiences of individuals. Susan Heathfield (2017), a human resources expert, describes it as follows: "Culture is made up of the values, beliefs, underlying assumptions, attitudes, and behaviors shared by a group of people." It incorporates the unspoken and unwritten rules and is learned through interactions. Culture surrounds us and culture extends to the virtual environment. Most organizations want to make a serious effort to extend their culture to the virtual environment.

Leaders in an organization have a profound effect on culture because of the role they play in setting objectives and carrying out day to day operations. The language they use, the symbols they hang on walls, the stories they tell and their daily work practices implicitly or explicitly set the tone and the culture. A controlling culture automatically sets the tone for a lack of trust. The reverse is also true. Lack of trust sets the tone for a controlling culture, directly or indirectly. Power is not connected to control, not in the 21st century. Power is connected to ideas and knowledge. The general operational norms for a group, things like great customer service, attention to detail or support and caring for employees, are all elements of culture and can greatly influence the performance.

People are more than commodities. They have hearts, emotions and minds. Most organizations don't pay enough attention, if any, to the ideas of their people. Ideas are way too often treated like a problem and a threat. Management says they want innovation. They may even have a program or two on critical thinking skills and innovative thinking, but deep down in the culture is a fear that anything different is disruptive. Disruption is a lack of control. A lack of control is a threat to management. Most management spends a great deal of time pushing and trying to enforce their own ideas of time, agenda and speed of execution. There is little support for people to innovate, think or act with autonomy and very little trust.

People feel powerful when they have the power to create ideas and enact their priorities. They feel powerless when they need to check in with others all the time. This is not collaboration. This kind of incessant communication is based on control, not transparency and not cooperation. It squelches intrinsic motivation. It takes the excitement and enthusiasm out of the contribution. Taking away a person's autonomy by insisting on falsely motivated communication discourages creative thinking and innovation. This is probably not where we want people to be mentally. Creativity is not a problem, not a waste of time and certainly not a threat. Even though most new ideas are not acted upon, it takes a lot of them to find the few that will really be awesome.

It is very important that the ideas of virtual workers are honored. The virtual workplace needs to support the knowledge worker and their creative ideas. Interactions between coworkers and the freedom to live life as well as to work can inspire that creative spark to get things done. Freedom is one of the reasons people want to work virtually. Give them room to move, the freedom to challenge the status quo and the support they need. The more they contribute and have their ideas accepted the more buy-in organizations receive. People feel good when they contribute. They feel important, needed and involved.

The virtual workplace is a dramatic change not only for the individual but also for the company culture. It is more difficult to make sure that people are acting out the ideas of others. It is also more likely that people just won't do it. They will remove themselves physically, mentally and emotionally if they do not feel like they have some "skin in the game." This is true in a F2F environment also, but because of physical presence it can take years, sometimes even decades, before anyone notices.

Change starts with YOU! Each manager should take it upon themselves to support and encourage workers in the virtual workplace. Create touchpoints to reach out and inspire and generate an environment that encourages creativity. Each touchpoint is an opportunity. The virtual workplace will not support old and ineffective ways of doing things. Eventually and sometimes painfully these practices will be dissolved. False rhetoric is not tolerated. Legislated control will result in turnover and unhappy, uninspired and unproductive workers. Each touchpoint is the way we can support a virtual worker.

Start with a touchpoint plan and connect. Isolation and absentee management is not connection. Criticism and confrontation, even if it is subtle and indirect is not supportive. Sarcasm, complaining, ridiculing, correcting, reprimanding and in general putting people down or in their place just won't cut it. If we want to encourage people in the virtual environment, we need stay positive. Create positive energy and keep them involved. Get them to talk and ask them questions. Support the individual and their ideas and take and make the time to listen to people. People know when you are really interested in them and when you are faking it. Get real. Pay attention and establish emotional and cognitive connection with every encounter. And tell people, with positive regard, how important they are to the success of the organization. Choose not to encourage this kind of supportive environment and the organization will pay a price.

Multicultural Conflicts

Multicultural virtual teams can place special demands on leadership. Conflicts that arise from cultural differences can be subtle and hard to identify. Disagreements over delivery dates and strategies can become personal quickly and create feelings of mistrust and anger. Multicultural virtual teams can create challenges and dilemmas for management. The challenge is to recognize the underlying cultural differences and to intervene in ways that keep the business objectives front and center and empower the team members to meet those objectives (Brett, Behfar, & Kern, 2006).

Company culture can make or break success in the virtual workplace. Leadership in the organization plays a big part in setting the tone and establishing a culture of trust, mutual goals, and respect for and the value of each person. To support the virtual workplace, the organization and the individuals within the organization in roles of leadership need to value the virtual workplace. They need to understand that it is here to stay and that individuals and creativity can flourish in this environment for many reasons. A culture of control will not support all the elements that make the virtual workplace a great place to work. The values, beliefs and underlying assumptions will be based on mistrust, not creativity and support. The rules and the unspoken behaviors will be based on "us against them," 20th century industrial economy logic. (Heathfield, 2014).

Don't underestimate the importance of symbols in the virtual environment in supporting this dynamic. Do employees have what they need? Do they have a positive representation of the organization in their personal work environment? Do they have things with the logo, branding and reminders of their importance and connection? Do they have clear communication channels? Are there boundaries and limits in place? Does the organization respect the individual and their right to privacy? In many ways, the virtual workplace is like a startup organization. Communication is one to one and touching people is personal. Communicating is essential and needs to be explicit and intentional. People who do well in the virtual workplace need rewards and acknowledgement, and those that do not need us to be open, honest and communicate clear expectations (McKinnon, 2013).

All change to organizational culture requires participation and cooperation on the part of the employees. Clayton Christensen et al. (2006), in an article for the Harvard Business Review, The Tools of Cooperation and Change, discusses different tools to achieve cultural change based on the type of organization and agreed-upon results. He discusses tools for power, management, leadership and culture. The tools that will be the most effective in the virtual workplace are the management and culture tools. Power and leadership tools, not so much. Management tools focus on process and coordination. Cultural tools focus on a deep consciousness of priorities and a set of actions that will allow a company to achieve those priorities that are clearly communicated. In other words, clearly communicated priorities and expectations are essential to the success of the company and the individual.

We can't change organizational culture without knowing what the organization wants and what needs to change. Most importantly, to create a culture that supports a productive virtual workforce it takes planning and effort to ensure that the desired performance becomes a reality. People need to replace old values, assumptions and behaviors with new ones. This starts at the top and requires a commitment from leadership. It takes training...and then more training. One workshop on the virtual workplace and communication planning is not enough!

Communicating to employees what is expected is critical to success. The organization should train managers to develop performance objectives and effective communication plans that are real and shared. These plans need to be regularly evaluated and revised with input from the virtual worker. The virtual workplace requires commitment and processes to ensure success. The final note on this topic is that organizations need to look at their current systems and infrastructure and ask if these are supportive. Work systems such as employee promotions, pay practices, performance management, hiring, training and development, and internal support resources need to be evaluated to see if they are applicable in the virtual workplace (Heathfield, 2014).

GlobalNet is an international software developer that provides custom products for high end networks. The company was asked by a client to produce a custom solution very quickly so they assembled an international team to get the job done. The virtual team had members from Brazil, Mexico, Japan, India and the United States. From the very beginning the team members could not agree on a delivery date for the product. The team from the U.S. said three to four weeks and the Indian team members said three to four months. As time went on, the project fell further and further behind schedule. Team members were reluctant to point out the delays and setbacks. Jim, the project manager, would only find out about these when it was time for the work to be handed over to him. As tensions mounted, things became more personal and tempers flared. Conflict over day to day, even mundane, issues became difficult. Team member communication continued to break down. Jim became so inundated with operational details and decisions that he was drowning. It was well past even the predicted four months when Jim decided he had to do something.

Jim: "I went to Japan to meet with the development team there and they literally put me in a closet. I was in this tiny space with a desk and a computer. It was very clear that I was not a part of the inner circle and they did not want to work with me. They did not even want to talk to me unless they really needed to. I was totally unable to discover what was going on there. All I know is that I am frustrated and this project is falling behind big time."

Aiko: "He was not really interested in what we had to say. We go to the virtual meetings but he is always in the lead. He doesn't really want to discuss

Case in Point: Global Net, Inc.

Meet the Staff

73

anything. He doesn't want our feedback or our expertise. He feels that because we are not as fluent in English as he is we are not as intelligent. One of our programmers who barely speaks English is the expert in his field."

Carlos: "I speak English pretty well but sometimes I don't feel like I have the words to say what I want to say. When I go to virtual meetings with Jim, he does all the talking. All I do is listen. This is understandable but disappointing. My team is really good and we have important input. I am also at the same level in the company as Jim."

Fernando: "I tried to ask questions. In Mexico, you grow up learning to ask questions. You are supposed to be humble so you ask questions that are open ended. This is out of respect, not because you are stupid or don't know the answer. Jim thinks I am an idiot and don't know anything. He thinks I really don't know what I am talking about."

Jim: "After the last meeting, I felt a little better. We had agreed on three out of four points. I was ready to start on point four at our next weekly meeting. Carlos was too, because I talked to him but then the Indian team wanted to start at point one again! They wanted to go back and discuss the whole thing. I almost had a heart attack. This really is not working."

1. How do different cultural norms make the participants feel?

2. Have the team members been treated disrespectfully? Do you think this can influence the course of the project?

3. What does hierarchy have to do with culture?

4. How does this play out in different cultures?

5. How does it play out in your culture?

6. Why does cultural difference get personal?

7. Which strategy is better, adapt or exit?

8. What are your attitudes about direct and indirect communication and the part they play in your culture?

1. Describe an event or a circumstance that recently made you very angry or upset because a situation seemed to be unfair or unjust or just wrong.

2. External stimulus triggers a reaction. What triggered the event?

3. Emotion is created and spreads through the body. Thoughts are called up based on this feeling. What did you feel?

4. Describe the belief behind the thoughts.

5. Is that belief true? Is it rational? Was is conscious?

Exercise 2: Expressing Your Company's Culture

Write down 15 words that most accurately describe your company's culture.

1.

2.

3.

4.

5.

6.

7.

8.

9.

10.

11.

12.

13.

14.

15.

Please answer on a scale of 1 to 4, where 4 is strongly agree, 3 is agree, 2 is disagree and 1 is strongly disagree. (The highest score possible is 80 and the lowest score possible is 20.)

Exercise 3: Virtual Employee Engagement Survey

1. I know what is expected of me and I have clear priorities at work.

2. I have the everything I need to do my work right in the virtual workplace.

3. I am in touch with my manager at least three times a week and we usually talk every day.

4. I receive praise and recognition for doing good work almost every time we talk.

5. There is good job/work-related communication.

6. There is good job/work-related communication between myself and my manager.

7. I am proud to work for my company.

8. My company provides me with provides me with opportunities to acquire new skills and knowledge that will assist in my professional growth and development.

9. My manager clearly communicates what the company is trying to accomplish (corporate goals, objectives, etc.).

10. My manager provides me with timely feedback and constructive advice when I need it.

11. My manger is competent in his/her job.

12. I regularly interact with senior management at least two levels above my boss.

13. My manager cares about me as a person and my life.

14. My company encourages my development and makes promotion and career paths a priority.

15. My coworkers are committed to doing quality work.

16. I know I am important and making a valuable contribution.

17. I have a close friend at work.

18. In the last three months, someone at work has talked to me about my performance and progress.

19. I know that what I do is important to the company's progress and mission.

20. The compensation (including base salary, PTO, health benefits, other benefit programs, summer hours, etc.) I receive is appropriate for my job and level.

Exercise 4:
Cultural
Expectation
Analysis

1. What are the expressed and unexpressed expectations in your organization's culture? Is it the same in all departments?

2. How do these cultural expectations influence leading in the virtual environment?

3. What conceptual influences exist in your organization (intangibles, branding, shard perceptions, views, semantics and dialectics)? Do they support working in the virtual environment?

4. What transactional influences exist in your organization (mission statements, performance requirements, process manuals, organization charts, information systems, political structures)? Do they support working in the virtual environment?

5. What actual influences exist in your organization (interactions between workers, leaders and workers, leaders and leaders, infrastructure, performance tasks)? Do they support working in the virtual environment?

During much of the Twentieth Century, management and workers were paired off like fighters in a ring, at opposite ends and pitted against each other. The desires of management were productivity and profit. The desires of labor were wages and benefits. This opposition dictated a lack of trust in and a lack of concern for the individual. Profit and loss were important, powerful and real. The feelings and experiences of the individual were discounted and irrelevant. When you were at work, what was important was to get the job done. Nothing interfered with work. Feelings, personal experiences and life happened after 5 PM. Western business culture segregated work and life. Then technology came along and changed all that. The objective world of work and the subjective world of life merged.

In the virtual world, work and life can be blended. This blending of work and life creates a new experience for the worker and the manager. The subjective experience becomes as important as the objective one. Both parties are trying to synchronize experiences to meet a common set of goals. In order to determine the experiences a person is having in the virtual environment, leaders want to learn to listen intuitively with intention, listening with the intention to respond in a way that validates not only what should be done but also affirms a person's internal frame of reference. In the virtual environment, the individual's frame of reference is very important. The results of listening with an intuitive perspective are that both parties can grow. The virtual workplace can promote satisfaction and accomplishment for both business and workers if both parties are willing to cooperate, collaborate and focus on results.

Chapter 4

Listening Between the Lines

The most important thing in communication is hearing what isn't said.
—Peter Drucker

Listening in the virtual environment is tuning into the intent as well as the commitment of the other party. Working in the virtual world requires management and workers to listen very closely to each other. Listening involves more than just paying attention. In a virtual environment, this can be challenging. Virtual environments can have great deal of noise, both internal and external. The environment itself is connected but detached. Virtual workers report feeling more productive but also experiencing more disturbances and interruptions. They are influenced by but detached from the corporate culture. Virtual workers value the flexibility and autonomy of working remotely but fear they are not being heard, are going to be overlooked for promotions or are invisible to management.

Virtual managers can have concerns about their influence and control. They value success and fear their lack of physical presence may result in poor worker performance, unmet objectives or inferior results.

Four Steps to Effective Virtual Listening

There are four basic steps to effectively listening in the virtual environment: active listening, reflective listening, responsive listening and intuitive listening. Active listening is the first step and requires focused attention and concentration. Reflective listening acknowledges the speaker and confirms an attempt to understand the message. You check your understanding by mirroring or restating what you think you heard. Responsive listening shifts the dynamics and opens the door to new possibilities in relationships. It acknowledges that the person is in charge of his/her own life, supports autonomy, and trusts that the objectives of the individual and the organization can be aligned to support mutually beneficial results. Intuitive listening validates and confirms the importance of the person's position and his/her intentions. Intuitive listening helps a person accept responsibility for their own experiences and feelings and it acknowledge that these are within his/her own control.

Active Listening

We learn to distinguish between personally significant and insignificant information almost from birth. Teachers will say that students are not going to learn if they are not paying attention. Often, paying attention requires active listening. Active listening seems so easy but requires careful focus and mindfulness. Research suggests that we pick up sounds associated with personal and emotional relevance very quickly. We all have preferential processing of personally significant information. Examples of this kind of information are if someone calls your name, if your device rings, or if you hear your child's voice.

The brain is built to tune in or tune out very quickly. Most of the time when this is happening you are unaware of it. When your device dings, your email pings or your phone rings, it is easy to be distracted, lose focus and not actively listen. We are all human and this is how most humans are hardwired. Your brain has the ability and will change how it will respond based on what has happened in the past. If our meeting or our coworker was boring last time, or we thought the interaction was insignificant, we might just tune out.

Studies conducted using animals suggest similar results. Animals remember behaviorally relevant information and sounds by storing a memory code in the cortex. These are then activated depending on the motivational value of the stimuli. In other words, if it is something the animal considers motivating they are more likely to tune in. The more important the sound, the more specifically tuned the response becomes. We all have these experiences with our own pets and children. When you open the treat cabinet, the dog goes bananas, but when you say clean your room, your kids just don't hear that. People selectively tune in, or not, often without being aware.

Voluntary attention is not a prerequisite of active listening. This is important. Incoming information is matched with what exists in our memory. Specific, personally significant and behaviorally relevant stimuli are matched with templates stored in our brains. This matching mechanism begins with the onset of a sight, sound or smell and involves experienced-based neural connections that go beyond sensory processing. Increased involvement leads to a more widely spread neural network and increased synthesis of neural activity. The more we are involved, the more actively we are likely to listen (Roye et al., 2010). Active listening can be cultivated. These skills are extremely important, but our educational system spends very little time teaching or cultivating them. Studies suggest that nearly half of us lack active listening skills. Active listening is the first step towards effective and intuitive listening.

We use auditory methods (written or oral) to communicate information most of the time. When we compose text messages or emails, we are communicating using writing. Listening, writing and speaking effectively are critical communication skills. Sending, receiving and understanding virtual communication requires us to master these skills.

We have all received a message with incorrect spelling or poor grammar and focused on the mistake, but is that what we want to listen to?

Our culture assumes that children and adults know how to listen. This assumption is not supported by research. In the virtual environment, it is important to produce context specific feedback that reaffirms our understanding and comprehension. Distracted listeners often produce affirmative feedback but seldom use feedback that is specific or set in context. In the F2F environment the responses of a distracted listener can be detected by a different pitch, more headshaking and less intensity. If we much are using live videos to communicate online, distracted responses will be very like F2F responses. If we are communicating asynchronously, a distracted listener might use simple responses that are friendly, affirmative and detached like OK, K or Got it, but lack specific information and context.

What does it take to be an active listener? It starts with a general willingness to respect the potential worth of the other individual. Carl Rodgers and Richard Farson from the University of Chicago coined the term active listening in 1957. In their landmark article, they discuss the importance of considering the insights of other people and trusting people to have the capacity to be self-directed as absolutely imperative for effective listening. In other words, if the listener comes to the conversation with the position of "I'm right, you're wrong," effective listening is impossible. Rogers and Farson also picked up on the fact that when people are listened to, they tend to listen to themselves more closely, which puts them in touch with their own feelings and thinking. Active listening then is not only a way of receiving information but it is also a way of influencing the other person's autonomy. Active listening supports independence and brings about positive changes in people.

A willingness to adjust our attention to absorb what is relevant and stay positive encourages understanding and comprehension. This is active listening. Active listening requires concentration and focus. In a F2F environment, we rely on making eye contact, nodding heads and body postures. Both verbal and nonverbal behaviors influence dialogue. We confirm our understanding by asking questions, repeating, rephrasing and not interrupting. Common pitfalls are tuning into someone's voice, stance or demeanor rather than the idea's being presented. Our affections or emotions act like a filter for our attention, attitudes and willingness to adjust. Some people will augment their listening efforts by writing things down or asking themselves questions to increase focus and attention.

Active listening doesn't insure that what is being communicated is what is being heard. "What I think I said is not what I think you heard" is a common problem brought about because we all construct our own thoughts and meanings. Metacognition is a term used to describe "thinking about thinking." We construct or make meaning out of our thoughts by evaluating what we take in. We incorporate new information by associating it with what we already know. Meaning depends on prior knowledge and how we associate new input with what we know. We reflect on new information and ideas that are the same or different than our own. This evaluation cannot take place without active listening skills. Active listening is effective listening. Active listening is a way of listening to other people that improves mutual understanding (Campbell, 2011).

One of the things that makes active listening so powerful is that it does not threaten the individual's independence, but rather supports it. Trying to change others through influence and threat only increases defensiveness. Your image of "self" and your beliefs are very deeply ingrained. So deeply ingrained that in many cases you believe these thoughts are facts. It is easy for you to accept and integrate experiences that support the image you have of "self." When you have other experiences that do not fit with this image of self sometimes you don't accept or admit to these at all.

Real changes can only be made by the individual who is aware and wants to change. If the conversations are perceived as threating, there is little chance of effective communication. Part of the reason for active listening is to create an atmosphere that fosters genuine communication and decreases threat through criticism, evaluation and judgment. Threat triggers the fight or flight response and doesn't support autonomy.

Active listening challenges demands for decisions, judgments and evaluations. Judgment of any kind causes freedom of thought, creativity and expression to shut down. Even well-meaning advice and information is an attempt to change a person and can cause disconnect. Common techniques of communicating often fall short when it comes to active listening. In conversations, we are all asking for verification of our ideas, plans and concepts. We ask people to agree or disagree with us and to validate our own point of view. Many questions or challenges are only masked expressions of emotions or perceived needs. Because as complex human beings we are unable to communicate these emotions openly, we often disguise these feelings to ourselves and others

Developing active listening skills requires a willingness to get inside the speaker and grasp his/her point of view. This means an inside out approach. We want to understand the content of the topic and also the emotional or underlying attitudes. Both are import and both give meaning to the message. Let's look at an example. Say a worker comes to a virtual meeting and reports "I have finished that project." Now listen again. What if the worker says, "I have finally finished that damn project?" Same content... different emotions. Taking time to listen actively is the first step on the ladder to listening with intuition. The meanings in these messages are totally different. Say the supervisor responds to a work situation by just giving another assignment to the worker. How does that worker feel? Did he/she get her point across? Does he/she feel respected, validated, appreciated? Does he/she feel good about completing the project?

Beliefs are our foundations for reality. We all have our own set of perceptions, preconceived notions and beliefs. We react, defend and validate our beliefs to reaffirm that what we believe is indeed the only truth. When you believe you have to influence and control outcomes this can translate into "I have to influence and control others." You believe you should fix situations, make people feel better and defend your agenda, so it is very difficult for you to listen to another person, especially virtually, when the connections tend to be shorter, less frequent and more indirect. You may have been taught to push your own points, say what you think you need to, and assume that this is all it takes.

When we communicate virtually, often the communication is written. Although active listening was developed for F2F communication, it works very well in text messaging and email, but it takes a little more effort. Part of successfully acquiring active listening skills is being able to see the results. If the other party perceives that we are actively engaged and listening, we are well on our way (Bauer, Figl & Motschnig-Pitrik, 2009). Active listening builds to reflective listening.

Reflective Listening

When you are developing your listening skills, you want to remember that the content of the interaction is much less important than the feeling behind it. One way to help identify with the feelings of another is to reflect those feelings back to the person. The meaning and the message are linked together. By reflecting, we not only acknowledge the person but confirm an attempt to understand what the message is all about. We want to reflect not only the words but the words and the feelings the other person is delivering. This makes listening an even more important tool for dealing with human behaviors. If the person talking thinks the person listening Is only playing cat and mouse, then listening will not be very effective. When we reflect back the conversation, we are saying "I acknowledge and understand your point of view," which doesn't necessarily mean we agree with it but does give an indication of understanding.

Reflective listening is not a skill most of us have. It can be acquired. All it takes is practice and willingness and it also might require a change in attitude. We want to acquire and convey a sincere interest in the other party. We can reflect in our own words what the speaker seems to mean. This is often called the mirroring technique and means exactly that, reflecting back to the speaker what you heard him/her say. We can restate the speaker's words aloud, in writing or both. It is the communicating back to the speaker that is important. The ground rule for this is that before we make a point of our own or state something new we want to reflect the point or position of the other person (Rogers & Farson, 1987).

Reflective listening requires us to take the point of view of the other person and define the problem and solution from there. It enhances our relationship because it shows we are interested and trying to relate. This gives us a shot at trust and respect. Confrontation, on the other hand, usually shuts relating down. It is difficult for people to admit they are wrong so when we reflect back what the other party said we are showing respect and building understanding. Asking questions, rather than making statements, is always a good approach. Questions are open-ended and statements are absolute. We want to move out of it is my way or yours and into mutual understanding and an agreed-upon approach.

Above all else we want to resist the urge to argue. The temptation to be right and want to be right at all costs is normal for most people but fight it. Keep the conversation open by dodging and weaving. There is an old Charlie Chaplin movie where little Charlie keeps taking small little side steps and outmaneuvering a very large boxer. Eventually the boxer just gets tired and gives up. We might want to try the same approach with reflective listening. We want the other person to come to their own conclusions. It is much more powerful than telling. In reflective listening we emphasize strategically, try to establish a common ground and delay giving our opinion unless it is asked for repeatedly.

What we are working toward is empathy and genuine appreciation for the other person's point of view. Leaders want allies not adversaries. By establishing an interest and a dialogue we have opened the door. In the virtual environment, it is as much about process as content. Content is everywhere. Process can be cut short. We want to keep the conversation going.

Here are some signs you might not be listening reflectively:

- You discover yourself interrupting the other person.

- You feel like no one is paying attention to you.

- You find yourself name calling or engaged in self talk.

- You are using adjectives that are very unflattering.

- You are bringing up things from the past.

- You are bringing up issues that are not related.

- You are arguing.

If we are involved in a conversation where we are interrupting the other person or the other person is interrupting us, we are much more interested in making our point than listening. This is especially challenging online because there are fewer visual cues. Remember the purpose of reflective listening is to try to take the perspective of the other person. If we are arguing, we are more interested in being right and saving face, especially if there are other people around. When this happens, it is very unlikely we will be heard. If it gets to this point we want to step away and calm down.

Online we have to rely on our self-control to turn down those heated emotions. Try to end on a positive note. Take a breather and rethink your approach. Step away from the conversation. Try something like, "I would like some time to think about this. Would you mind if we talk about this later?"

The point here is to get some distance and give yourself a chance to regroup.

The point of reflective listening is to let us identify our real goal, to get off the power trip and forget about how right we are, and to keep our conversation focused on communicating and creating a relationship. Ask a lot of questions. Reflective listening is an active process and requires active listening. The sole purpose of reflective listening is so that we can respond and not react. If we reflect back to the other person an understanding that does not include controversy or criticism, the other person will not think we are an adversary. They are more likely to be open and willing to establishing a trusting relationship with us if we are listening. Online, relationships are very important.

Responsive listening changes the way two people relate. It shifts the dynamics of control and opens up new possibilities. Connecting with other people virtually takes skill. Active listening and reflection are only the first two steps. Responsive listening is being willing to let go of your own ideas and delivering and defending your own agenda so that you can identify with and validate the other person's ideas at least enough to connect with them.

Managers often feel the need to function as the judge and the jury. This sense of judgment of the person or the situation as either good or bad or right or wrong sets up our interactions. If we judge the other person as good, we want to connect with them and we value their input. If we judge them as bad, we want to defend our own position and find ways to diminish their input. This sets up the paradox of control. The paradox of control is believing that we can control others by speaking and acting. In reality, we can only control ourselves. When we want to control the outcome and defend the cause, we find strategies to attack or attempt to change the other person. When we want to connect, we want to get closer to the other person, support them and collaborate with them. Listening and waiting are more powerful but less obvious ways to gain influence. The important point is that to respond and not react we need to be present.

Presence is the only way to experience empathy with another. Empathy is a critical ingredient in understanding. Sympathy seeks to control but empathy requires a certain degree of emotional distance. Responsive listening requires stepping out of the ring long enough to detach from anger, fear and anguish. Responding is about overseeing our thoughts and therefore our feelings. If we are defensive, we may be experiencing anger, fear, pain and/or desperation. It is very difficult to manage strong negative emotions and respond in a way that supports connection. Empathy gives us the distance to respond and not react, which is the first step to aligning our connections (Gillies, Pan, Slater & Shawe-Taylor, 2004).

When we use responsive listening, we listen for particular material. First, we listen for emotions, feelings and emotional experiences. This puts us in touch with the persona at a very different level than just understanding the facts. Second, we listen for self-concept. This is how people view themselves, with a focus on self-evaluation. Finally, we listen for motivations and defenses, wishes and fears by tuning in to the dynamic elements of the conversation and connecting the dots. We want to identify the state of a person's "identity capital" which tells us "how they do what they do and who they are."

Many times, we are listening for things the person may not be aware of themselves. These underlying self-concepts are internal and exist within every person. However, and this is important, we do not listen with the idea of associating or judging in any way what the other person does or how they feel with internal motivation such as passions, desires or meanings. Our reason for listening responsively is only to determine what exists. Responsive listening is interested in listening for the self-concept without judgment.

Responsive listening considers that people are complex and not isolated. They are composed of the self and then influenced by the dynamics of the systems in which they interact. The person affects the system and the system affects the person. The person directs interactions but these are not caused by solely by internal feelings, emotions or other motivations. The self-concept is interacting with other mental representations and influenced by these representations. Our concepts, transactions and interactions influence our intentions. For example, when two people have a conversation they interact. What takes place in that interaction is influenced by the words they use and how they use them. We interact with others and with our own mental representations. How we do this is guided by our intentions.

Responsive listening also realizes that not all interactions are guided by the objective world. For example, we start to think about lunch and a restaurant we want to go to for lunch. The restaurant itself is in the objective world. It is brick and mortar and it exists. When the self creates a mental representation of this restaurant it is an objective representation. However, when we start thinking about how we felt the last time we were there we are no longer thinking objectively. We remember the waitress who was so nice and complemented us, the friends we ran into and the great lunch. We are in the realm of emotions and experiences. We are creating an interaction with the restaurant that is both subjective and experiential. Responsive listening tunes into these differences. It realizes that what is being represented is usually a mixture of objective and subjective interaction.

Intuitive Listening

Talking and listening are both interactions. Talking is an interaction with the listener and listening is an interaction with the talker. In the virtual environment, these interactions can be both synchronous and asynchronous. Synchronous transactions are traditional and direct. They happen with both parties in the same time and space. Asynchronous transactions are the result of ever expanding communication technologies and can be instantaneous but are always indirect. This presents certain challenges. We are constantly involved in and reacting to, if not responding to, the world to fulfill our intentions. When we are removed from the person we are talking to, either by space, time or distance, the transaction between the talker and the listener is more likely to be influenced by our interpretation of it. In other words, what we are hearing is more predisposed to our own feelings, meanings and intentions. What the other person is saying is also predisposed to their own "self-state." Intuitive listening then is tuning into the cohesive connections of the feelings, meanings and intentions that are being represented by the interactions.

Intuitive listening combines our ability to experience and reflect on interpersonal meaning with our ability to make decisions and initiate action. When we use intuitive listening, we are not separate from the interaction. How we interpret and act are all part of an executive system. This intuitive executive system responds to mental representations and responds with intentional interactions with the world, other people and their actions. Intuitive listening requires a shift in position. In the objective world of facts, we operate based on "me." In the intuitive world we operate in the subjective state based on "I." In the "I" state we create our own meanings, feelings and implications. Intuitive listening requires us to play the role of the initiator.

Me and I are very different representations of reality. Things happen to me: technology breaks down, people need me to do things, and my power goes out. I respond or react. I feel stressed, I have a sense of responsibility to others, and I feel confident the power will be back soon. When I respond, I am initiating the interaction; when I react and I am allowing someone or something else to. When we listen we have mental representations, anticipations, objects, feelings, perceptions and self-talk going on in our brains and the other party does also. Intuitive listening opens the door to intuitive interpretation. Simply rephrasing statements from "they did something to me" to "I did something" will open doors for intuitive listening. When we are the initiator, we control our actions and reactions. When we are the object, we are the victim. In the virtual world, it is much too easy to react.

Let's look at an example. Suppose it has been a long day. We were up early and in the office and from the time we started work things were just difficult. We couldn't find a file we needed, our email box was jammed with trivia, our project is behind schedule, our team member sent a text and is sick again, etc. These are all interactions with the objective world, our representation of circumstances and what other people have done. If we are in the "I state," perhaps we are feeling tired, discouraged and a little anxious. We might be thinking: "I am really stressed. I need a vacation. I really feel exhausted." If we are in the "me state," we might be thinking "this is just not fair" or "nothing is going my way". We might mentally be talking to the team member, the computer or the company with statements like "He/she is sick again. This is the third time this month and it is always on a Friday. He/She knows we have a deadline and we are behind." Or... "That damn file, I know I saved it somewhere, there is just too much stuff on this hard drive!" Or... "This is not fair, it is not realistic. This project schedule is too much." In one case we are tuned into ourselves, and in the other case we are listening to the world.

We all go back and forth between the "I "and the "me." You do and so do the people you work with. Having the ability to listen and respond will put us in a good position to move into intuitive listening. Because the virtual environment lacks cues, we want to be more insightful and perceptive. We want to learn to listen between the lines to what others are saying and to what we are saying to ourselves.

The virtual environment is one of dichotomies and contradictions. We are connected to our team but we are continents away. We are responsible for the outcome, but we can't observe people's behavior. We are not supposed to be working, it is 10 PM on a Saturday, but an email just came in and we feel like we must respond. We fluctuate between meeting the demands of self and meeting the demands of the world.

In the virtual environment, the behaviors and tasks that are traditionally considered to be supportive of the company have changed. We don't go to the office, we can work from almost anywhere and we live in a world that doesn't start at 9 AM and end at 5 PM. In a traditional environment, the captain runs the ship. In the virtual world, the individual runs his or her own ship. The captain and the crew have changed places. Without the support of the company and management, the virtual workplace cannot exist. The organization provides direction, resources and situations. Management needs to meet and adjust to new and ever-changing circumstances. But it is the individual's job to steer his/her own ship. Intuitive listening will help us tune into to where our ship is headed.

Intuitive listening allows us to tune into the other person's sense of self, their purposes and their level of self-reliance in trying to accomplish goals, task and objectives. It helps us discover the confidence or lack of confidence the other person possesses in their ability to get things done. If the person perceives themselves as an object of the world, the recipient of experiences they cannot control or influence, they are likely to experience negative feelings like guilt, judgment or fear. This often results in a feeling of helplessness, anger or shame at the inability to meet the standards of others. Understanding the individual's self-sense and self-reactions can alert us to the perspective. For example, "I really don't like the fact that the deadline has been changed again" is really not about the deadline but about the person's reaction to the deadline. This interaction has a goal. The goal of the interaction is to let us know that the person is upset. If we intuit and understand the real goal, we can appreciate the interaction (Zimring, 2000).

Intuitive listening lets us understand the direction the person is moving. Is it toward a solution or an excuse? By listening for the quality of the feeling that the person is trying to convey what is happening, intuitive listening lets us understand the goal, the purpose and the intention of the interaction. Suppose our team member says "I am really stressed right now. I lost my babysitter and I have to take the kids to my mother's house. She is willing to take them but she is very unpredictable with how she treats them. She is not really reliable." What is the goal of this interaction? What is this person trying to tell you? How do you discern the goal? Then your team member adds "I am looking for a new babysitter and I think I will find one soon." This is what we respond to. We can see that he/she is trying to really find a solution. He/she is a little uncomfortable with the current situation, but we support that effort. The intention is to find a workable solution.

Learning the four steps to effective virtual listening has beneficial effects. Better listening skills support growth and change lives. When we feel like we are visible, supported and listened to, we are more likely to act with autonomy and make responsible choices. We ask a great deal of people in the work environment. In the virtual world, individual initiative and autonomy are not only supported, they are required. Learning to listen well enough to respond to someone's intentions and experiences requires practice. Most people are not born with these skills and have not been taught them in K-12 or K-20.

In the virtual world, success means autonomy. Autonomy is about living our life for our own purposes, setting and enacting our own priorities, and being authentically productive so that we intentionally get things done. The company is not in charge. Acting with autonomy means a person oversees themselves. We govern our own life. The objective is to achieve results. The worker is not helpless, delinquent, untrustworthy or trying to get over on the company. The company is not only interested in profits, outputs, balance sheets and cutting costs. In the virtual environment, it is a partnership. A partnership that must be built on mutual understanding and support. How we create interactions requires thought and attention to intention. Interactions that are right in front of us and part of our daily life are available to us. In this way, we validate ourselves and others. This helps us all to attain mastery over ourselves and our lives.

Case in Point: Janet Johnson

You just get off the phone with Janet Johnson. Your conversation is summarized below:

"Janet! How are you today? I'm glad to hear you are doing well. I just wanted to follow up with you to see if you completed that proposal for the new client I promised them by Friday. I know how hard it can be for you to get everything done with your mom and the kids at home.

Ms. Johnson says "No, honestly I haven't even had a chance to look at that mess. You keep giving me more to do every week. My mom was sick and had to go to the hospital and everyone is focused on helping her get better. I am not really worried about that proposal right now. I know it is important though."

You can feel yourself getting angry. You agreed upon a deadline. Can you believe this? Doesn't she put work first? Does she want to keep her job? It seems like she cannot accomplish anything. You have half a mind to just tell her, her job is on the line. What do you do? What conversations do you have? Where do you start?

1. How do you use active listening techniques? **Questions**
   Reflective? Responsive? Intuitive?

2. Create a conversation between you and Janet
   Johnson that uses these techniques.

3. If possible, get a colleague and role play this
   conversation. Then switch positions and repeat.

4. Identify the benefits from this approach for
   leading and inspiring better performance.

JoAnn works for The Protective Insurance Company. She processes claims and works for an hourly wage. She has never met her supervisor. She is a good worker and usually works the night shift because her husband is ill and at home. She has been working virtually for about two years and feels comfortable but lonely. She really has no other choice in her situation because her husband has a long-term illness and she is the caregiver. She never misses work and usually does what she is supposed to do. She makes her claim quotas. But lately she has been missing in action more and more. She calls in sick more often and some days she just doesn't get it all done. Her boss has noticed because his boss has begun to notice. Let's look at the conversations.

Meet the Staff

JoAnn: "I am doing everything I can. I try I really do. It is just that George has been sick for so long. Sometimes I wonder if he is ever going to get well. I try to keep my spirits up but I am not sure how much more of this I can take."

Kevin: "Now of course you can keep your spirit up and hang in there. You have done well in the past."

JoAnn: "But it has been so long. It seems like the doctors don't know what they are doing."

Kevin: "You know that the doctors know what they are doing. George has great doctors. You shouldn't be questioning his care. This shouldn't interfere with your job."

JoAnn: "Well he certainly is not improving like he was supposed to and I just have a hard time concentrating. I am exhausted all the time."

Kevin: "How long has he been sick?"

JoAnn: Seven months.

Kevin: "You really should get out more. Sometimes things just take time. I think it might be a good idea to have someone come in and stay with George at least a few days a week. Maybe then you could get out and away a little more. Then you'd be able to focus on your job."

JoAnn: "I don't want to get out. I want him to get well."

Kevin: "He will get well. He has good doctors. You need to focus on your job."

Contrast this to the conversation JoAnn has with Kevin's supervisor, Bill.

Bill: "I understand you talked to Kevin last week."

JoAnn: "Yes I did. He is concerned because I am missing so much work. I tried to explain that my husband is sick and it has been a long road and he still is not well."

Bill: "It must be heartbreaking to see your husband so ill."

JoAnn: "It is. Sometimes it feels hopeless. Mostly I just feel like I have to handle this entire thing myself and I get no relief."

Bill: "You seem really discouraged."

JoAnn: "It is just so hard." (JoAnn begins to sob and her voice cracks.)

Bill: "Is there something we can do to help you?"

1. Why is Kevin having such a difficult time with getting his point across? In what ways is he placating? In what ways is he glib? In what ways is he judging? In what ways is he probing?

2. What kind of a reaction does JoAnn have to Kevin's conversation?

3. Why is Kevin's advice met with resistance? How do you think JoAnn feels after this conversation? How about Kevin?

4. What does Bill do that is different? Where do you see active, reflective, responsive or intuitive listening taking place?

**Exercise 1:
Active Listening**

The average person speaks at about a rate of 150 words per minute (wpm).

The problem is that we can hear at about a rate of 1,000 wpm. This obviously gives us a lot of extra time.

1. What do you do with this extra time?

2. How hard is it for you to focus on what the person is saying?

3. Focus on how the person is saying it?

4. Not formulate a response while the other person is speaking or you are reading an email? Acknowledge the content only?

5. Not interrupt or finish the sentences yourself?

6. How might you develop active listening skills?

Exercise 2: Reflective Listening

Get a partner. One person assumes the role of the communicator and the other becomes the listener.

The communicator: Tell a story about something that you really liked that you heard about in the last week. The listener: using these five key areas reflect back what the communicator said.

- Paraphrase the message

- Repeat the message

- Inquire about missing information.

- Clarify any points not completely clear

- Remember the important points.

- Switch roles and do it again.

Check those habits that might interfere with your ability to listen responsively. Be honest!

- I assume I know best.

- I interrupt often or try to finish the other person's sentences.

- I jump to conclusions.

- I am often overly parental and answer with advice, even when no one asks me for it.

- I make up my mind quickly often before I have all the information.

- I am a habitual note taker.

- I don't give any response afterward.

- I am impatient.

- I lose my temper and discount or get angry when I don't agree.

- I try to change the subject to something I can identify with.

- I formulate my reply while the other person is speaking.

- I am not really concerned with what the other person says.

115

- I get easily distracted.

- I tune the other person out.

How many checks do you have? Now take each item checked and write down a new practice that will allow you to develop responsive listening skills.

No communication is communication. Explain why not being in touch with workers in the virtual environment really sends a strong message. What might it be conveying? Is this only true for people in positions of authority? Why is it as important to compliment as to correct? Chose three words commonly used in conversation and list at least four different meanings for each word.

Exercise 4: Intuitive Listening

Example: Common

shared common property; common interests

belonging equally to an entire community

inferior quality

ordinary, widespread

Now, role play a situation and discuss the difference between objective and subjective meaning. What cues are you using to be intuitive listeners in the virtual workplace?

Inspiring Performance in the Virtual Workplace

Communicating virtually means communicating differently. It requires leaders to develop new skills to build strong relationships. Not only do they need to be able to listen with intuitive skills, they also need to be able to communicate on a one-to-one level. Leaders need to listen more deeply and communicate more personally. This helps in order to detect what is being left unsaid in an email or determine how life elements are affecting employee engagement. Goals need to be more clearly defined than in a F2F workplace, and expectations need to be conveyed and measured. About 40% of current work can be done virtually. Working virtually means working differently. It requires a different set of skills whether you are the captain or just one of the crew.

The virtual workplace offers freedom and cost savings to both employer and employee. It comes with inevitably greater responsibilities and the need to self-manage. Most research suggests that when virtual employees feel empowered they also feel the most engaged. The virtual workplace can be a driver for empowerment and engagement but it can also be a lonely place and very isolating. Strong interpersonal communication skills can help us to empower workers and make them feel more connected to a community and dedicated to meeting organizational objectives.

There needs to be more informal conversation and social conversation. Being a leader in the virtual workplace requires more tolerance, willingness and ability to cope with change. It requires a willingness to lead in a more extroverted way than in a traditional workplace. Leaders in the virtual space simply cannot afford to be aloof, reserved and detached (Haid, 2010). Since the 1980s when we all

Chapter 5

M2Y Connections: FROG

My belief is that communication is the best way to create strong relationships.
—Jada Pinkett Smith

became connected, there have been three major waves of virtualization in the workplace. The first wave was the freelancers, the second was the virtual colleagues and the third is virtual coworkers.

The first wave, the independent contractors, led the way in virtual freelance work. Consultants and experts who never really had to be inside the four walls of the organization were now able to work virtually and set up a one-person shop. This was embraced by organizational culture and the freelancers. Stay at home parents, retirees, caregivers, part-timers, students, and other talent could "telecommute." This gave organizations the ability to hire at will. It allowed people who could not work because of their physical proximity to return to or stay in the workforce. As technology evolved so did connectivity. Flexibility and real-time collaboration became part of the mix.

The second wave was an exodus from the corporate office spurred by freedom. Although working virtually often meant giving up job security, benefits, healthcare and retirement, workers left in droves during the second wave, looking for freedom and a flexible schedule. With the promise of autonomy and a better work-life balance, not to mention shorter commutes, the people in the cubicles started to work from home a few days a week. Senior executives struggled with a world that was going global and new ways to measure and evaluate performance. Technology kept improving and many organizations like IBM took the lead in supporting a virtual workforce. By 2009, IBM's virtual workforce grew to about 400,000 contractors and employees.

The third wave was a wakeup call. The joke was that IBM stood for "I'm by myself" and business began to realize that there was a difference in the virtual workplace. Many virtual workers felt isolated. Collaboration was more challenging. The focus shifted from how can we do this to how can we do this well. Interactions with other people, collaboration, flexibility and isolation were the buzz words. Then the light began to go off and again the technology improved. A new focus on collaborative meetings, communities of practice and guild-type practices began changing the mindset. Human resource departments began to realize that 24/7/365 connections could be stressful and affect employee wellbeing and work/life balance. The insecurities of not having people physically at their desk caused panic and irrationality. Measuring achievement became paramount. In the third wave, we finally began to realize that the technologies were the easiest part of working virtually. Human communication, feelings and empowerment had to be redefined (Johns, 2013).

Most communication in the virtual environment is one to one communication or me to you (M2Y). This is how it feels anyway. Knowledge is shared and there is a feeling that nothing is absolute. Reality is something that is constantly being negotiated and renegotiated. The virtual environment demands a certain kind of openness and trust. It is more informal and demands more collaboration and discussion. It is clear that one of the important elements for success in the virtual workplace is getting people to collaborate and cooperate, which means that communicating clearly and openly to build strong interpersonal relationships is a skill that virtual managers need to acquire. We participate in discussions with coworkers we really don't know and share thoughts and ideas we used to keep to ourselves. It also requires people to self-monitor and self-regulate, which are skills that many people have never learned. But more than just collaboration, the virtual workplace requires cooperation and reliance. The communication is flatter and more evenly distributed. Cooperation supports higher achievement than competition or individualism (Bell & Koslowski, 2002).

But how to do it? Many people have never learned the art of communication. We are challenged in the virtual workplace to communicate effectively. How do we make conversation in an environment where we are disconnected? Where we are often communicating with strangers? The skills and confidence to strike up a conversation can be lacking. Research suggest that lack of conversation confidence and skills is one of the biggest roadblocks to affective virtual communication. Of all the skills necessary to be a successful leader in the virtual environment, communication and conversation skills are some of the most helpful. Understanding that there is a need for interaction and that listening as well as question and answer exchange taking is far more effective than either one alone. Being able to recognize some basic virtual communication tenants and employ a simple technique known as FROG will go a long way to towards building communication confidence and strong relationships (Pepe, 2013).

The Communication Sandwich

The biggest mistake people make in communication is telling not asking. Information and feedback are both a part of communication. The information sandwich technique is a three-step process that makes information easier to swallow or take in. The first step is to ask permission, step two is to provide the information and step three is to obtain feedback or clarify. Why do we need to ask permission and how exactly might we do that? Asking permission breaks down barriers and gives the other person a juxtaposition in motivation. Instead of demanding attention, we put the other person in the position of inviting us in. This gives them a sense of control and breaks down defenses and barriers. It makes the other person feel like they have more control of the situation. It makes them more comfortable. Simple introductions like "Can I ask you a question?" or "Is it okay if I express a concern about this?" sets the tone for the conversation.

The second step is one that we are all used to, providing the information. The challenge here for many of us is to stay open and to provide this information in a non-demanding, non-threatening way. It is easy to fall into patterns of communication we may have learned years ago and come up naturally. These are communication traps. If we can learn to avoid them, we have a better chance of getting a conversation going.

The Sergeant Friday Trap

"The facts, Ma'am, just the facts," as Sergeant Friday use to say back in the 1960s. We are taught from the time we are little that if we have the facts that is all that is important. You can't argue with the facts. Unfortunately, we all have different perspectives and see the facts differently. There is no objective reality. All reality is subjectively filtered through each of our own unique perspectives.

The Teacher Trap

"I'm going to tell you, tell you again, and then tell you I told you!" I will talk at you and you will take it in and understand exactly what I want you to. I know more than you, I understand more than you. Therefore, you must listen to my every word and believe everything I say. If not, I will continue to lecture you until you get it.

The Blame Game This is where we make it, whatever it is, the other person's fault. Blame is a sure way to shut communication down immediately.

The Right or Wrong This is where we take a side and the other person is wrong. There is no room for discussion. Once we take a position the other person may naturally take the opposite position just out of defense. Now we have a right and a wrong and no conversation. Or we ask a question where there is only one possible answer. Closed questions will shut conversation down the same way.

The third part of a communication sandwich is feedback or clarification. Don't overdo this step. Some people have a habit of saying "Do you get that?" "Do you understand?" "Does this make sense to you?" This can be an annoyingly dismissive part of the conversation. It is however, important to ask for feedback and check for understanding. Feedback is about acknowledgement and conveying understanding. If you don't understand, ask. If you do understand then let the other party know.

FROG: Family, Recreation, Occupation and Goals

FROG an acronym for Family, Recreation, Occupation and Goals. Remember the most important word in drawing someone else into a conversation is you, not me, not I and not myself. What FROG does is shift the focus from you and your concerns and interests to the other person. Everyone has heard the expression "It's not what you know but who you know and how well you know them!" Connecting, networking and knowing the right people are the first steps on the road to success. It comes more naturally to some people than to others. We are not all Bill Clinton by nature.

Information is everywhere and it is nowhere. Facebook, Google and Apple control a great deal of what we see and how we see it. We trust less and connect more. We have thousands of friends on Facebook but fewer than ever in real life. We send emails, texts, and voice messages. There are more and new apps and devices that communicate every day. For all the texting and messaging we do we really have fewer solid and trusting relationships because technologies filters so many cues. One on one F2F interaction still has the biggest impact on getting to know people and letting people get to know us.

If we focus on asking questions in this area not only do we connect but we get to know people. This allows us to take a genuine interest in people, and in the virtual world that is important. Genuine needs to be emphasized here. People will pick up on a phony even online. Asking questions about FROG allows us to break the ice. It gives us a way to open the conversation and draw someone in. If we are dismissive and insincere, we will do more harm to our relationship than we will do good.

Use FROG with tact and discretion. The old saying never mess with a person's family, home or money has validity. We want to convey interest, not come off as a busybody, gossip or "nosey Nelly." Treat people the way they want to be treated and be aware of their boundaries. If we pick up on signals that this is something they are not interested in sharing with us, we drop it. What's important is to connect with people on a personal level and build relationships. Remember to stay positive. If the only time our virtual coworker is hearing from us is once a week at the project management meeting and all the news is negative that isn't going to keep anyone connected. Don't be afraid to pick up the phone, jump on video chat or have a F2F meeting. Text is informal and direct, and email is formal and indirect. Focus on the other person and make the connection.

The entire point of FROG is to get away from talking just about the business and the problems. We want to get to know this other person, even though we are connected virtually. We want to help him/her be the best they can be. FROG is what virtual leadership is all about. Do not communicate in a way that is controlling, berating, or panicking. Leading in the virtual world is about empowering people to be engaged. When we finish with the conversation, then what? What are the action items? Focus on finding something we can do for the other person by the end of the meeting, conversation or chat. Remember not to dominate the conversation, but to engage in it. Questions are the key.

If we use FROG to start or continue the conversation, it can be much less threatening. FROG can stimulate conversation. We will shift the emphasis from us to the other person and come across as interested and confident instead of detached and threatening. We really have two options. We can either ask the questions that invite the other person to speak or we can make a statement that is intended to get them to contribute a response. Questions are an easier and more open way to move the conversation forward. They invite interaction and feedback or insight. Questions allow us a clear and a direct path to figure out what is going on. We no longer need to guess, be a mind reader or a fortuneteller.

Another thing to remember is that everyone talks to everyone else online. We don't want to focus on criticism or judging but instead concentrate on curiosity. Understanding why things are happening will get us a lot closer to results than judgment. We want to watch our emotions, especially negative emotions. Just because we feel badly we really don't want to make our coworker feel badly. We want to talk with someone, not at them. FROG can help us to communicate intentionally. Remember that how we communicate virtually has a huge influence on engagement and satisfaction. Trust comes from communication and building relationships. The more people trust us the more they are willing to do for us. The more they are willing to do the greater they are engaged.

This may take some practice because the RAS (or Reticular Activating System) part of our brain controls what you focus on. If we have been self-focused for a long time, it takes practice to focus on the other person. Using FROG and a commitment to better virtual communication will help. We don't want to be afraid to praise someone and tell them they are doing a great job. We don't want to assume they know it. We want to always say thank you early and often, especially in a virtual environment. It is important for people to feel appreciated. When we are disconnected and isolated, feeling appreciated can go a long, long way.

We also don't want to be overly reliant on email. We can't really listen with email and we can't give or get direct feedback. Email is formal (top down) and indirect. Keep your communication positive, funny and interesting as much as possible. We don't want to confuse online communication with a visit, a call or a card. We want to make our communication as personal as we can and keep it appropriate. FROG is a tool to help us focus more on others and less on ourselves. The more we engage others and take care of them, the more they are willing to do for us. Then the problems and numbers begin to take care of themselves.

We want to remember that all people have unique communication styles and personalities and be attuned to how people are listening and interacting. We can use our intuition to pick up on what is being said and what is not. We don't use a broad yet superficial style of online communication. We want to focus more deeply on less quantity and more quality and be aware of overwhelming coworkers with too much. Remember that quantity is not quality and certainly not engagement. Using casual language and focusing on FROG helps. Allowing conversations to grow and build by asking questions and having others contribute their ideas keeps the conversation moving and focused. We want to listen to what our virtual coworkers are saying and look for their motivation. The rule is to listen early and often and provide feedback, and support when we can.

Empathy in a relationship leads to connection and usually success. FROG helps us to dissolve alienation and isolation. It is important in a detached and isolated environment to know that someone values us, cares about us and takes an interest in our life. Communication that is accepting and nonjudgmental will help us to build relationships that are closer and stronger. This in turn will help create engagement and trust, two of the most important aspects for success in the virtual workplace. FROG gives us a way to connect. Listening with empathy gives us a way to build and sustain real bonds and relationships online. Tuning in to what people are saying and "feeling" gives us insight into their perspective.

Case in Point: The Bunker, Inc.

The Bunker, Inc. is a web informatics company that does one thing, it collects and stores data. It doesn't do anything with the data, it just collects it and archives it for other companies. There is a lot of complaining going on at The Bunker. The employees keep getting mixed messages. One well-meaning supervisor tells them one thing, and then another tells them something else. Imagine you are the person in charge of the employees and supervisors described below. As you read this case, give special consideration to how clear communication and FROG might be helpful.

Meet the Staff

Ben works at the main data center in New Jersey. He is 47 years old and is responsible for managing the staff at the data centers and all of the employees. Each center has about four employees and runs twenty-four hours a day. They all work from home, but come in when they need to. Each center is functioning pretty much on its own.

The employees are between 21 and 65 years of age and for some English is not a primary language. These people come from diverse cultural and ethnic backgrounds. Ben has an M.S. in Data Analytics from Penn State. Most of his staff have high school diplomas. Some have graduated from college, but all have received special training from The Bunker on data storage, backup and integrity.

Ben developed a new process and a checklist that looks for missing data. The company executives are supportive of Ben's efforts to an extent. They also understand that these extra efforts cost the company money.

Ben is also going through a very difficult break-up and some issues at home. He comes into the office sometimes a little stressed, and when he communicates on the webcam, it can look like he just woke up. He can be very short tempered. He also hasn't been out to visit the virtual data centers in a long time.

The Bunker operates 24 hours a day 365 days a year. When someone takes a day off, someone else makes up the shift. The employees are required to monitor the data that comes in and fill out some transaction logs. The workers are hourly and have very little contact with each other. Despite the efforts Ben has made, which include emails with subjects like: PLEASE COMPLETE LOGS and BE CAREFUL/BE ACCURATE, there are still a lot of mistakes.

Questions

1. What are the challenges Ben might face? What challenges might the data center workers face?

2. What are your suggestions for solutions to these challenges?

3. What are some of the communication challenges Ben might face? Generational? Cultural? Language?

4. How might Ben use "FROG" as a motivator for employees?

5. What might Ben do to build relationships that are stronger? Based on trust?

F- Family

- Where are you from originally?

- How is big is your family? How any children? Boys? Girls?

- How many brothers and sisters do you have?

- What was the favorite holiday at your house growing up?

R- Recreation

- What do you enjoy doing for fun?

- What did you think about the Valley High basketball team this year?

- What's your favorite football team?

- What's your favorite movie this summer?

O- Occupation

- What did you do before you started this job?

- What do you enjoy most about your work? Why?

- What would you do if you could do anything you wanted?

- What is the most challenging part of the job?

Exercise 1:
How to Create
a FROG
Conversation and
Role-play

G- Goals

- What's the biggest thing you want to achieve in life?

- If money and time were not a problem, what would you like to do?

- Are your goals different now than when you were younger?

- Where do you plan to take your next vacation?

Now grab a partner and try FROG out. Then reverse roles and answer the same questions. Did you learn anything? Do you feel closer to this person? Do you feel like you know and can relate to them a little better?

Exercise 2: FROG Talk

People who have run virtual projects, been in charge of virtual teams and own or manage organizations that have large virtual workforces understand that when you deal with people in the virtual space you need to be able to trust and listen to "your little voice." Managing people in the 21st century means managing people virtually. Leadership and management is caught in a fast-paced and changing world. The tension and stress created by dynamic change often leaves managers struggling for meaning, purpose, and direction and leads to irrational and erratic thought. They need to develop a balance between the rational and the sensitive, the analytical and the intuitive ways of thinking. The more we move toward a knowledge-based and service-oriented society the more we rely on humans to assure success.

Leading in the virtual world requires the ability and commitment to building relationships that are trusted, positive and reliable in spite of barriers like the lack of visual and emotional cues. Often these relationships are with people who are cultural opposites, inherently different or basically antagonistic. Doing what is right and what is fair is a matter of perception, and perception is a unique quality subjectively developed on an individual basis. Leading in the virtual workplace requires more self-knowledge, self-regulation and emotional balance than in the F2F environment. It requires leadership to take an interest in and make a strong effort to support worker success.

Establishing trust, one of the key elements necessary for success in the virtual workplace, comes from collaboration, shared expectations, missions, vision and engagement. This can range from mutu-

Chapter 6

The X Factor

There is no logical way to the discovery of these elemental laws. There is only the way of intuition, which is helped by a feeling for the order lying behind the appearance.
—Albert Einstein

ally agreed upon project goals and timetables to expectations about performance, hours, and delivery schedules. Virtual leadership and virtual workplace performance requires a high level of collaborative skills, a demonstration of trust-building, higher levels of communication, and extensive support and dialogue to support engagement and success.

For much of the 20th century, business and organizational leadership focused on ROI (return on investment). Business and workplaces used the "Big Three," time, money and quality, to measure and evaluate everything. Leadership in the 20th century could be broken down into three categories: the laissez-faire (hands off, non-leadership leadership), transactional (give and take) and transformational (good behavior is coaxed or inspired by the leaders from the followers). Leadership approaches that ranged from the transactional to the transformational all relied on being present to evaluate the results. We either ignored what went wrong and were only passively interested in supporting workers after the fact or fixing mistakes after they happened. Leadership sometimes took a more active approach of looking for errors and ignoring what went right. The transactional style had well-defined rules and roles and consequences.

Transactional leadership appeals to many because it is impersonal and nonjudgmental except for the results. It takes a perfectly detached view of the "self" and eliminates and discussion of our internal desires, preferences or paradigms.

The transformational approach focused a little more on the individual and less on conveyor belt mentality but still left a lot to be desired. The leader was the role model who coached, coaxed, inspired and motivated the followers. Transformational leadership appeals to high levels of motivational reasoning.

The 21st century brought a new way to view leadership and interactions called "authentic leadership." In the virtual workplace, authentic leadership aligns very closely with the "respond-abilities" detailed in The Pajama Effect. This is not a hierarchical view of leadership but one that is inclusive and practical. Authentic leadership says "walk the walk, don't just talk the talk." Authentic leaders are hopeful, positive, resilient, confident and collaborative. They build relationships and have the self-discipline to get results. They are open to development and change. They establish and maintain close relationships with people that are supportive and are perceived as contributing to the success of others. With strong relationships at the core, they create communities and positive social exchanges. The virtual workspace has led to a convergence of management and leadership ideologies and out of necessity forced the replacement of theory with practice.

A 360-degree view of interactions and contributions has dominated this area, so 21st century virtual workplaces are about stakeholder engagement for all parties involved. Effectively engaging and influencing others requires a totally different skill set than traditional management routed in the industrial age. The knowledge worker and virtual workplace rely on conscious thoughts and responsible actions. They function best when people know themselves well enough to take responsibility for their own behaviors, paradigms, limitations and eccentricities. They require workers to be able to act with autonomy, set and enact priorities, be authentically productive, make responsible choices and align their connections. Authentic leadership is about behaviors that support worker and organizational intentions.

It takes effort to build relationships online. In the virtual workplace we form alliances, build relationships and align connections. Virtual workers share risks, opportunities and rewards based on trust and agreement. Cooperation and collaboration are essential if the mutually agreed upon outcomes are to be achieved. Soft skills, communication, emotional intelligence and intuition play an important role for authentic management and employee engagement. Authentic leadership is reliant on intuition and is built upon mutually agreed up on values, commitment and trust (Lloyd-Walker & Walker, 2011).

A Brief History of Intuition and Leadership

Intuition as a valuable part of leadership and management started in the 1930s with Charles Barnard. Bernard was the President of New Jersey Bell Telephone Company. He was a practitioner not an academic scholar. Intuition apparently went latent as a practice for about 40 years and then reappeared in leadership, management, psychological, learning, educational, risk, morality and a host of other forms of literature. Bernard, however, is given credit as the first management writer to openly refer to intuition as a critical component in job roles. He believed that mental process fell into two categories, logical and non-logical. He argued that leaders didn't always have the luxury of making decisions based on ordered and leisurely rational thought but often had to rely on intuitive responses because of circumstances that required fast decision making and complex judgements.

In the late 1940s, Herbert Simon was the first academic to really examine the link between intuition and management. However, as an academic his work was not applied in practice. He felt that in a business environment human behaviors were intended to be rational but weren't always. He looked at intuition through the lens of domains of specific expertise. This approach resonates with later work that has pattern recognition playing an important role in intuition theory. Characterized by familiar cues, intuition is an outcome of a reaction to and interpretation of situations. Simon did not rule out the possibility that the subconscious or unconscious might be a better decision maker than the conscious mind. Later contributors to the field of intuition and leadership point out that intuition is greater than just pattern recognition and add that it creates and combines elements to form new solutions and interpretations. Herbert Simon earned the Nobel Prize in Economics for this work in 1978.

Daniel Kahneman and Amos Tversky arrived on the scene in the 1970s and brought with them the "down side" of intuition. Kahneman and Tversky explored human bias. Their research was devoted to the systematic exploration of judgements and choices based on intuitive errors which came from false interpretations and misconceptions inherent in human mental processing. They looked at intuition as thoughts and preferences that enter the mind quickly without much reflection. Intuition fell somewhere between the automatic operation of perception and the more thoughtful and deliberate operation of reasoning. They gave us heuristics that represented the downside of rational cognition. Three of the main ones are representativeness or "what is typical," availability or what "easily comes to mind," and adjustment and anchoring which means "what happens to come first." A great deal of research and publications about the implications of their work spread from psychology to fields as diverse as medicine, law, politics, economics and business administration (Akinci & Sadler-Smith, 2012).

Another approach to examining how humans process information sprung up about the same time and is known in many circles as the "neuromyth." Popularized by Daniel Pink in his book A Whole New Mind: Why Right Brainers Will Rule the Future, Pink argued that left hemisphere or analytical and strategic thinking was going to be replaced by right hemisphere or creative and relational building, none of which was based on research or facts. This train of thought began in the early 1970s with Henry Mintzberg, who declared that planning was a left hemisphere operation, and management was a right hemisphere operation. Planning was logical, analytical and verbal but management was creative, intuitive and imagined. None of this was based on fact either but was his view that good management was as much of an art as it was a science.

Much research has been skeptical and very critical of these views. Criticisms range from the approach being unproductive to just plain lying. In 1987, Simon made two strong points on intuition research that debunked the right and left brain approaches: 1) research does not in any way imply that either hemisphere independently is capable of problem solving, decision making, or creative discovery; and 2) for performance and organizational behaviors, it is the behavior that is important not the hemisphere. At best the approach is considered a metaphor for two different ways of thinking.

By the 1980s, intuition research was becoming more mainstream and many streams of thought were evolving. Contributors included Mintzberg, Isenberg and others and focused on senior management and how leaders think. The conclusions generally centered around thoughts like "the higher you go in a company the more important it is to combine intuition and rationality" (Akinci & Sadler-Smith, 2012).

From the 1990s to the present, dual process theories have dominated. Thinking Fast and Slow by Daniel Kahneman and The Power of Habit by Charles Duhigg are two examples of books that reflect the current paradigm that the brain contains two systems. System 1 processes are context dependent, automatic, unconscious, about associations, implicit, fast and intuitive. System 2 processes are rational, independent, rule-based, and generally slow. Emotions are generally thought to be part of System 1. The affective domain or the emotions have become part of the mental processing models. Intuition is now looked at as combining the dynamics of the situation, both affective and cognitive, and using experience to recognize certain patterns. Experienced professionals can make decisions and perform high stakes tasks under time pressure by relying on their ability to recognize problems as similar to problems they have experienced previously. Intuition is now recognized as having a component that is automatic and is effected by affective as well as cognitive processing in the brain.

From 2000 onward little has been done that doesn't include feelings and emotions as part of intuition in leadership and management. A non-sequential information processing model replaced the hierarchical model of input, process, output, storage (HIPOS), which dominated the 20th century. Models now explore non-sequential processes that arrive at a direct knowing. These models often combine cognitive and affective elements without conscious reasoning. Intuition, which was thought to be scientifically weak and on the fringe, has arrived as mainstream. Much work is being done on problem solving intuition and on creative intuition. STEM (science, technology, engineering and math) is being replaced by STEAM (science, technology, engineering, art and math) in school curriculums as an attempt to foster new thought patterns. There has also been a focus on moral intuition and associated outcomes.

Modern brain mapping techniques and neuroscience, although in their infancy, have given us a glimpse at associating insight vs intuition. A lot more needs to be done in this area, and with the help of ever more impressive technologies the work continues. As we move forward with the role of intuition in many disciplines, it becomes clear that it is very valuable and needs a lot more exploration. This however should not keep us from using it or developing it to our greatest ability. Especially in a virtual workplace, intuition plays a very important role to connecting with and staying abreast of developments that are dependent on the art of leadership. Therefore, using intuition is increasingly important as we move into the 21st century and more and more people are working away from the office. We need to spend more time reflecting about how we engage with others and become more aware of our intuitions and how we integrate them during the decision-making process. Kahneman proposes we are not likely to doubt our own intuitive responses unless reflective processes have been engaged.

Accessing your intuition and trusting it comes easier to some people than it does to others. In order to access intuition, it is necessary to reflect and realize that you are using it intentionally. When one consciously manages the impact of those personal feelings by recognizing, understanding and questioning one's own biases and beliefs, it is possible to begin to govern one's own intuition. Making the unconscious conscious is done through reflective engagement in order to recognize feelings, emotions and thoughts and to develop a deeper insight into thought processing. Sometimes this involves checking and regulating emotions that have become automatic and entrenched. By examining multiple perspectives, some of which we may not agree with, we can increase our intrapersonal development skills and enhance our thought processing. Relying on our own intuition is all about developing intrapersonal introspection. Self-examination that looks into our feelings, attitudes, history and internal purposes is very important in governing and being able to rely upon our own intuitive processes (Schmidt, 2014).

Self-confidence and exaggerated self-belief can get in the way of reliable intuition. Some of us, for a wide variety of reasons, grow up with a contempt for advice and criticism by others. When it is unexamined, unchecked and unbridled, intuition can lead to narcissistic behaviors in leaders. "Intuitions are affectively charged judgements that arise through rapid, non-conscious and holistic associations" (Dane & Pratt, 2007) that combine thinking and feelings. Intuition requires a leap into the unknown. It is not part of a logical thought process and reasoning that ends in an appropriate conclusion. Therefore, intuition can be both useful and problematic depending on the use and the reliability. Your "little

Intentional Intuition

voice, gut feeling, hunch or vibe" sends a message to you to trust, select or act upon a particular situation or whether to distrust, reject or avoid it. But in order to rely on this "gut feeling" you need to trust that it is reliable. The more complex the environment, the higher the stakes with intuition. Intuition may continue to influence rational thinking and one must be aware that rational thinking can become a justification for intuitive reasoning. Instead of the rational thought being a check and balance on intuition, it can have very negative consequences. By mulling over or ruminating on internal thoughts that we assume to be true but are really grounded in bias, potential pitfalls and unintended consequences can emerge. Using a friend or trusted colleague as a sounding broad and getting a second or third opinion can help.

When your decision affects the lives of others, whether F2F or virtually, it is important to take the time to make sure that your intuition is reliable and on target. Leaders in the virtual workplace also need feedback. This is just another good reason to regularly do 360-degree evaluations. Sometimes when leadership is hierarchical and removed and receives little feedback intuition runs amuck. These leaders do not get a complete picture of the consequences of their actions and are more likely to use intuition inaccurately and indiscriminately. Often associated with narcissism or NPD, Narcissistic Personality Disorder, this is often associated with leaders like Steve Jobs. Jobs had a very strong reliance on his own "gut feelings" rather than getting help or receiving feedback. He said, "you always have to keep pushing to innovate." This may have come from an experience he had with Zen Buddhism in the 1970s.

"He attributed his ability to focus and his love of simplicity to his Zen training. It honed his appreciation for intuition, showed him how to filter out anything that was distracting or unnecessary and nurtured in him an aesthetic based minimalism" (Isaacsson, 2011).

Certainly, the three checks and balances usually associated with keeping intuition in balance, rational analysis, contemplation and external dialogue, were often missing with Jobs. Gates, on the other hand, appears to have uncoupled intuition to the point that he can reflect on it. Gates clearly has a high opinion of and trusts his intuition but tries to have a realistic view of what has worked and what has not over time. Consider this conversation Gates had with CNN:

CNN: Do you have some sort of sounding board to you use for when you see something that strikes maybe you as a good idea, but you're not really sure if this is going to catch on or is this really gonna be the big idea. Who do you ask?

Gates: Well, if I think something's going to catch on, I trust my own intuition.

CNN: And you're never wrong?

Gates: No, I'm often wrong, but my batting record is good enough that I keep swinging every time a ball is thrown (Claxton et al., 2015).

Educating and controlling your own intuition has an important role in leading, inspiring and measuring performance in the virtual workplace. It can have a profound effect on the governance, interactions and management of virtual workers and on institutional work polices and employee performance. When leader and workers are willing to engage in a reflective and analytical process that act as a check and balance on unbridled intuition, a great deal can be gained in the areas of trust, performance and engagement. Intuition promotes cooperation (Rand, et al., 2012).

Often the virtual workplace is missing or has blurred hierarchies, has a sense of flexibility and fluidity and a higher sense of uncertainty and risk. It is less stable and doesn't follow a traditional hierarchy of leader-follower constellations. Rather, the virtual workplace is an aggregate of individuals collaborating for a common goal, mission or cause. Virtual workers are more detached and isolated and therefore it is vitally important to establish common objectives and values. Traditional forms of rewards and punishments have little influence in the virtual workplace and are difficult to practice because of the lack of hierarchical lines. Relationship building is what replaces authority and what influences perceptions, values and commitment.

Relationships focus on people, their motivations, beliefs and behaviors. These virtual relationships are what support virtual workers in an atmosphere that is inherently seeped with a degree of uncertainty and change. Shared vision goes a long way to provide structure and engagement. Having a vision that supports outcomes and breaks down into tasks and aligns with goals that are clearly defined and detailed with specific responsibilities allows everyone to see the interdependence and reliability on each team member. Change always brings with it a certain amount of fear. Path and goal clarity and allowing room for discussion and individual autonomy and decision making is important. Because of the environmental uncertainty, leading in the virtual workplace requires building relationships that are certain, can be counted on, and are supportive and reliable (Tyssen, et al., 2013).

There is no room in the virtual workplace for what Jeffrey Pfeffer calls Leadership BS. Pfeffer, a professor at Stanford University, in his book, Leadership BS: Fixing Workplaces and Careers One Truth at a Time, indicates that power and politics continue to play a huge role in traditional organizations. Although leadership development and training across industry accounts for a cost between $14 and $50 billion a year, most of it is ineffective according to Pfeffer. One in every two managers is ineffective. Employee engagement and job satisfaction are at an all-time low. Most companies simply don't care about employee engagement and are more concerned with cost cutting because it has a quicker rate of ROI. Most of the time leaders look after themselves and not their people (Leavy, 2016). This type of leadership will be catastrophic in the virtual workplace. The virtual workplace relies on trust and once it is lost it is very difficult to reinstate it.

Intuition and Trust

Intuition and trust are closely related. Both are a way of processing information based on affect and personal standards. Both have a sense of automatic processing that cannot always be understood by rational thought. Knowing yourself and understanding your thought paradigms goes a long way in helping you understand both how you use your intuition and who and what you trust. When you don't have concrete information that allows you to use reasoning and analytics you are forced to use intuition and trust to make decisions. When intuition operates automatically it is usually through the beliefs and experiences of the individual. It can be biased and have unintended consequences if left unchecked. Intentional intuiting only happens when one engages in self-reflection and acquires a deep level of self-knowledge. Trusting your feelings and affective perspective can be developed through self-examination and practice. Intuition is not a choice and not a conscious process. It happens automatically, and reflection and expertise can increase the reliability of your intuition. Intuitive skills can be developed but it takes intentional practice and focus on your own personal abilities.

The best way to use intuition is to understand the process and use it consciously. Self-knowing and self-esteem are critical elements in intuiting. Intuition is not wishful thinking, insight or instinct. It can become a successful source of knowledge, guidance, strength and inspiration, and is an important element for leading in the virtual workplace. Remember that intuition is different in each of us and can be influenced by experiences, context and our own tendencies (Tonetto & Tamminen, 2015).

Case in Point: Almere Pharmaceuticals

The company you work for, Almere Pharmaceuticals, has decided to expand its training efforts for the sales representatives you have in Brazil. They want these representatives to be more motivated and increase their sales. You know that pride is a motivating factor for these representatives. They are spread out all over the country and most of them are in small towns and rural areas. Pride usually manifests itself in the form of family achievements and material accomplishments. This takes the form of cars and houses and college for the kids. Your little voice is telling you that you should collect testimonials from clients, most of whom are doctors' offices located in small villages and low income towns. These doctor's offices deal with people who have very basic survival needs and have many family issues to deal with. Although you know work accomplishments have an important place with the representatives you are not sure how this will play out with the clients. Based on your intuition you decide to go ahead with the initiative. These representatives will receive their end of year bonus in part based on client feedback.

Questions   1.   Do you think this initiative will work?

2. What role do you think work incentives play for the representatives? The clients?

3. Are their incentives the same?

4. How might you design an initiative that evokes pride in the representatives?

5. Is the target group similar to the representatives when it comes to work pride? What makes the difference? What are you assuming?

6. What might trigger emotion in the clients? How does that differ from the sales representatives?

7. Do you think you might need a different approach in other countries?

Exercise 1   What is your initial reaction to:

- Underage drinking

- College students taking drugs

- A single mother being deceived in a business transaction

- Your best friend who is married having an affair

- A virtual employee's computer has crashed again, the third time this month

- The death penalty

- The way your boss speaks to you

- Expensive gifts

- Being lied to

- Someone stealing your idea and taking credit for it

- Personal failure

- Discriminating against someone

- Hating your job

- Learning new things that take effort

- Feeling uncomfortable

- An employee wants to work from home three days a week

- Your employee seemed high when you talked to them

- A performance evaluation that is less than you expected

- Someone being always late

- Excuses

- Not meeting deadlines

Companies, organizations and institutions vary greatly in their commitment to support a virtual workforce. Some are great at developing and measuring learning that specifically targets virtual workers. Many are not. Some excel at identifying the challenges and strategies associated with performance development for virtual workers. Many are not. People who work virtually often feel unsupported, unrecognized and invisible. This is one of the biggest challenges currently facing employers. This chapter is specifically for those that struggle with this challenge. Supporting a virtual workplace goes beyond issuing a formal telecommuting or virtual work policy. Technology connects an interdependent group of individuals; however, it is collaboration, communication and sharing that allows them to accomplish common objectives. The virtual workforce needs to be supported with effective technology but also needs support in other areas.

Virtual workers meet objectives through collaboration, communication and sharing. Opportunities exist in each of these areas for organizations to support virtual workers. As organizations morph and grow, virtual teams become more and more important. Virtual teams are a common practice in many industries like technology, pharmaceuticals, healthcare and insurance. Organizations are waking up to employee demands and the realization that lower turnover, decreased travel and less mandatory relocation can have benefits for everyone. The business objectives are not so very different in this environment. Often, the business objectives parallel those in the F2F environment. They are, however, equally as important. Virtual workers need a clear idea of what the business objectives are and how their performance criteria align with meeting those objectives.

Chapter 7

Augmenting Autonomy

The best way to inspire people to superior performance is to convince them by everything you do and by your everyday attitude that you are wholeheartedly supporting them.
—Harold S. Geneen

159

Augmenting autonomy in the virtual workplace has its challenges. Management is not sure how to define what basic supervision is needed or how to replace spontaneous "watercooler" conversations. The "out of sight, out of mind" saying is just the tip of the iceberg. Virtual training struggles with technology, support, strategy and culture. Additionally, the current workplace is comprised of projects and assignments that are more complex and require a greater amount of knowledge. Adding to this saga is the reality that traditional approaches to managing people usually don't work in this virtual environment. So what is management to do?

A good first step is to recognize that this workplace requires continuous training and support to be able to achieve collaboration, communication and sharing. It is important to clearly define roles and responsibilities. We want to define how informal and formal communication will take place. Constantly updating our leadership skills including technology training, coaching skills, relationship and communication skills and emotional intelligence are especially important in the virtual workplace. The need to have virtual leaders who are trained and supported is evident. It increases effectiveness and efficiency.

This is an environment where trust is everything. Mistrust, misinterpretation, and uneven knowledge distribution make it difficult to collaborate, reach consensus and make critical decisions. It also makes it harder to carry out plans. By aligning connections and focusing on supporting independent thinkers, doers and contributors, it is possible to create an environment in which collaboration, communication and sharing exist.

Augmenting autonomy is challenging but it is also necessary. All workplace learning and development requires thought, investment and caring. It is not a once and done thing. Onboarding is only part of the learning and development process. Putting in the effort to train and develop workers helps with turnover, effectiveness and meeting key performance and ultimately business objectives.

Augmenting Collaboration

Collaboration is a byproduct of individuals coming together to move in a quest for purpose, direction and meaning. It is built on sensible, trustworthy and positive relationships. It is squashed by erratic behaviors, emotional outbursts and egocentric behaviors. Before you can collaborate, you need to be able to think independently. If I am afraid of what you think and dependent on your input for all my decisions, I am not able to collaborate with you, I am dependent on you. To have teams that collaborate, we must support individuals in acting with autonomy. Humility and an awareness of others intuitively supports collaboration. Collaborative skills can be learned through proactive practice but not until an individual can function autonomously.

Often organizations will avoid this area entirely because they feel individuals are too difficult to deal with. They will strive to hire certain kinds of workers and/or only let certain people work virtually. Undoubtedly, certain personality and individual characteristics work better in the virtual environment but everybody needs support. When companies value human beings as being important to their success, they realize that the investment in human capital has big payoffs.

Building relationships is key to encouraging collaboration. A culture that is innovative and aware values differences. Only then can leaders truly support workers, making connections and establishing relationships that are collaborative. Finding common ground between all sorts of things including race, age, ethnicity, religion, different functional units, culture and geographic regions supports collaboration.

To have collaboration, leadership must keep the communication channels open. Leaders need to be very highly involved in day to day practices. High involvement management helps to minimize uncertainty. It improves the perception of organizational support. Of course, this doesn't mean micromanaging, but it does mean knowing, caring and showing respect for the individual, the job they are doing and their accomplishments.

Augmenting Communication

The opinions workers have about the organization are formed by the communication the organization has with the individual. Communication is a strong part of high involvement management. More is not necessarily better. Communication removes ambiguity and defines clear expectations. Allowing workers to have more input supports clear communication by giving the worker a greater voice and therefore a greater stake in the outcome. Communication with virtual workers must go beyond the superficial. Perceived organization support is communicated by valuing adaptability, minimizing uncertainty and being forthcoming with rational reasons for change. When organizations carefully plan changes and communicate the reasons and impact of the changes it is possible to reduce uncertainty. Uncertainly can lead to fear. Fear opens the flood gates to a whole host of negative emotions. When the impact of decisions by leaders is clearly communicated and the expectations explained, it is easier to keep the communication doors open.

Communication can aid or hinder perceived organizational support. These influence attitudes and behaviors. Organizations are wise to take steps to ensure that the individual perceives the organization and leadership as supportive. When individuals are adaptive and open to change and supportive relationships, this comes through in their communication. Each individual can increase the organizational perception of stability and minimize uncertainty by identifying when they and or others need assistance and support in the workplace.

Augmenting communication can include feedback mechanisms, job rotation, 360-degree evaluations, training, rewards and recognition, socialization and other forms of engagement. We want to encourage workers to openly contribute. Actively enacting in and valuing this input decreases uncertainty and supports autonomy. It improves the perceptions of the organization as providing support for and valuing the individual worker.

Augmenting Sharing

Sharing information is another way to increase the perspective of support in the virtual workplace. This includes information needed to get the job done but goes beyond that. It includes organization appraisals which reveal stress and strain in relationships. These are not individual appraisals or performance reviews. These are at an organizational level and indicate the perceived level of trust, support and comfort experienced by a group of individuals across a defined area or the entire organization. When individuals perceive organizations as supporting, their attitudes and performance are different than when they do not (Cullen, 2014).

Worker perspectives provide an alternative point of view to the formulated opinions of management. This can create an avenue for open dialogue and positive change experiences. The perceptions an individual has of an organization influence job satisfaction and performance. Perceived support encourages workers to participate. They provide input to improve the workplace. Sharing organizations expect workers to maintain a positive job attitude and high performance. These organizations supply the necessary resources and training for them to learn new skills and procedures. Job satisfaction and employee performance can be directly linked to the ability to reach objectives and goals.

Virtual workers form positive impressions to the extent that the organization values them as individuals. The development a sharing and safe environment benefits both the individual and the organization. When employees feel that the organization is sharing, their social and emotional needs are met. When workers feel supported, they are more likely to have high job satisfaction, lower turnover and positive job attitudes. If their ideas are included it affects their disposition and interactions. These then influence others in the workplace. They set the tone for either success of failure. There is no question that working virtually is not right for every individual. The ability to work with autonomy, be adaptable and communicate clearly are part of being successful. Flexibility and adaptability go a long way to help the individual but the organization also has a role to play.

When leaders don't truly accept and provide support for the virtual workplace it often produces more stress for the virtual worker. Anyone who has ever worked knows the stress that can be generated when home or personal life and work priorities conflict. Too many demands and limited time can cause us to feel like we are letting someone down, either the company or ourselves. Working virtually comes with more freedom to set priorities but also with more responsibility. Virtual work policies are most successful when they are applied across the organization or department and supported by leadership. The perceptions of reliability, responsibility, dedication and dependability are changing as we progress but they are not changed everywhere.

Support can also come in a F2F form. It is important, when possible, to get people together in a F2F environment. Many studies support this. Spontaneous conversations, interactions, unexpected insights and possibilities can develop when people get together. Face time matters.

The industrial culture that supported 9 to 5 still exists. It doesn't matter what we do, surf the web or email friends, in many organizations being seen is still all that matters. The tendency to attribute productivity to longer hours in the office is often subconscious. It is one that leadership needs to overhaul. Organizations need to show widespread and uniform support for flexible scheduling. If workers don't perceive support, the virtual workplace suffers (Korkki, 2014).

More is Not Better

It is very easy to confuse quantity with quality when it comes to digital communication. Copying everyone on everything and texting folks at 10:30 PM or on a Sunday is a violation of privacy. Even on-call doctors get periods where they are off and can't be reached. Constantly being connected will cause stress and data fatigue. Virtual workers do not need to be reachable or accessible 24/7 to prove they are valuable. A policy of 24 to 48 hours for response time is usually plenty. If we really feel the need to have an immediate response, define the times and limit the exposures. For example, you will be available online Monday through Friday during regular business hours, EST (Eastern Standard Time).

When you live in a world that presidential policy is being convey by Tweets, it is difficult to set boundaries for communication, but it is necessary. There are just too many platforms, too much connectivity and too little self-control. You need to train virtual workers to understand what is important and ignore the bulk of correspondence that is insignificant. If it is important, make a phone call or Skype, do not have an email trail with more than 25 correspondences and expect anyone to follow it. Following email like this is like being lost in the ocean. Stop bombarding people with communication that is unnecessary and annoying. Stop being afraid you are going to miss something. Setting up some communication boundaries is an important way an organization can support virtual workers. It cuts down on stress and increases effectiveness when contact is important.

Setting limits is something the individual can do but the organization has to help with this.

It is great to believe that every leader has appropriate boundaries, but it is unrealistic. In a virtual work environment this can cause stress, burn out and turnover. There will always be exceptions to general guidelines. There are emergency situations that really do need to be responded to off hours, but those should be the exception, not the rule. When it becomes the rule it adds to stress. Like the boy who cried wolf, when everything is an emergency being constantly connected loses its appeal and effect. Urgency and meaningfulness become skewed when they are abused (Alford, 2015).

The main reason to set boundaries for constant contact is that all this connectivity can easily hurt productivity. The Pajama Effect discusses being able to align connections. In a world that constantly comes at us, it is not an easy task, but it is a necessary one. Organizations can help people learn this skill. Smartphones and devices keep us connected and engaged. They have changed the way we work and given us boundless flexibility. All this engagement can be distracting, especially if the organization and the worker have not clearly defined objectives and goals.

Study after study reveals that in a face-to face office or virtually, addiction to devices cuts into productivity. Here are some examples. Career Builder found that over 55% of people keep their device within eye shot all day long. Another study from University of Florida states that being pinged and dinged caused productivity to drop. Errors and omissions rise when workers are distracted. We have all been on conference calls or at a conference table when everyone is texting. It is annoying, distracting and most importantly it cuts down on productivity. In order to be productive, people need to be focused (Huppke, 2016).

Supporting people in a virtual environment means training not only those people but everyone who interacts with them. Organizations can offer training that makes people aware of this and gives them suggestions on how to focus. They can also create and adhere to policies that support boundaries. If the meeting is so boring that no one cares that the leader is rambling on, the organization can help to correct that.

The Importance of Ongoing Learning

Virtual teams require onboarding and ongoing learning support. To assure that morale, productivity and performance remain high, learning and development needs to be a part of that equation. Defining and training team members about team practices is part of what is needed. Virtual workers need personal, social, structural, technological and operational learning opportunities. Providing ongoing training in communication, coaching, and relationship building as well as technical or context specific skills also helps virtual workers be more productive. Organizations need to teach leadership about setting clear expectations and providing regular feedback. Through strategic hiring, providing learning opportunities and flexibility, it is possible for organizations to optimize productivity in the virtual workplace. Organizations cannot just tackle one area and ignore the others. Not if they want to be effective.

Social integration is of key importance to virtual workers. Leaving the virtual worker out hurts overall productivity. The more leadership is aware of the impact of leaving out virtual workers, the less it happens. Whether done intentionally or unintentionally, a reduction in formal and informal interactions can hurt. It is a balancing act. Communication needs to be inclusive and meaningful. Learning opportunities need to address the individual and the business needs. By focusing not only on contextual knowledge but also on the importance of interactions, virtual team training can enhance an environment that is void of cues and parameters.

With cues such as age, behaviors, style of dress and others missing, it is important to give people other mechanisms for establishing a person's prior knowledge and expertise. Virtual employees have limited access to teammates and the organization. Providing opportunities to synchronously engage is important. Social interactions require co-presence. Co-presence is based on responses and reactions. While asynchronous communication eliminates the constraints of time and space, they also diffuse the interactions between people. Social cues are eliminated and so are the responses that people learn when they learn to understand each other. Communication training, both formal and informal, helps virtual teams to be more productive, happier and more efficient.

The increasing number of virtual workers makes it important for organizations to examine what they are providing in the way of training and development. Onboarding for virtual teams is a good start but not the only learning experiences an organization should provide. In order to provide training and learning experiences that make sense for virtual workers, the organization and its leadership must understand the needs of all team members. There is a great deal of opportunity for creativity and exploration in this area.

Much of this is new and evolving as the technologies that connect us change. Areas that might be addressed are studying how these teams are onboarded and sustained. This research needs to go beyond technology and conflict resolution. How do virtual workers adopt to new team members? How does the organization provide ongoing support for existing and new virtual team members?

Data mining and analytics can give organizations much needed insight into where to focus these efforts. Qualitative interviews and observations still have an important role to play in indicating what the needs really are. All methods of empirical examination are important in order to give organizations insights for learning opportunities and performance improvement. Realizing that performance can be influenced by individual personalities and personas, group dynamics, socialization aspects, organizational policies (or lack of them) and technical and context specific content knowledge can help provide guidelines for performance success (Hemphill & Begel, 2011).

In a virtual environment, it may be more difficult to learn a team's processes and procedures. Often nothing is documented or if it is it is not conveyed. There is also the problem of a constant struggle between control and freedom, trust and doubt, and results and responsibilities. Information is communicated both explicitly and implicitly in the workplace. This is true of the virtual workplace as well. People need to be noticed and recognized for their efforts. One of the biggest fears of virtual workers is that they are invisible and will be passed over for recognition and/or promotions. In many ways, the virtual workplace requires a more hands-on, not hands-off, approach.

Visibility is important in the virtual workplace. If management is going to understand what contribution individuals are making, they have to establish normal expectations and how they are going to be measured. Setting clear performance expectations is essential. Tacit knowledge is conveyed from observation much of the time, so the good news is that in a virtual environment workers are less likely to learn from bad examples and negative coworkers.

In a virtual workplace, each person's work environment is different and unique. Although we assume that everyone is on the same page, pulling in the same direction and committed to the same cause, this is a big assumption. Preventing distractions becomes an individual's responsibility. We can believe that everyone knows what we know and sees what we see but perception is subjective. Documentation and dissemination of information helps to develop a more complete and up to date set of processes and procedures. Information that is usually transmitted implicitly can be shared.

Interactions in a virtual workplace can be supported with effort and intent. The frequency and nature of interactions in a virtual workplace have a direct influence on productivity and performance. By providing more structured processes and procedures and formalizing and documenting them, leadership can take some of the guesswork out of working virtually. By creating onboarding training, ongoing learning opportunities and addressing the needs of the individual as well as the organization, managers can set realistic and supportive expectations about productivity, time and connectivity.

Regular structured activities need to include the social and emotional aspects of the virtual workplace, not just reaching business goals.

Virtual workers need to be self-monitoring and proactive. They need to actively seek information and interactions. Social presence and social interactions in the virtual workplace make all the difference. The kinds of interactions individuals have, especially those that are informal and observable, are extremely important to virtual worker success. There is a great deal of opportunity for organizations to increase their efforts to support the virtual workplace. As technology continues to provide us with enhanced opportunities to work any place and any time, leadership in organizations needs to take on the challenge.

Case in Point: Besco Biotech, LLC

Besco is a startup firm in the biotech market. Besco is opening stores in London, New York, Toronto, Sydney and Los Angeles this month. Their goal is to have quick growth around the globe and take a considerable share of the market. They are customer focused and sales oriented. They have departments including business development, supply chain management, operations, and human resources. They are committed to leadership development at all levels. Their headquarters are in the UK but they have other new offices opening up in several countries. Besco is trying to identify what store managers might need to operate efficiently.

Questions

1. What questions might they ask? What kinds of resources might Besco want to provide for these managers?

2. What tasks might be business critical? What decisions might need to be made immediately?

3. How about the sales people? What might they need? The office staff? HR?

4. Why might it be important to define job performance first? How does job performance impact support?

5. What resources might Besco need to support management? Leadership? Are they the same?

National Office Supplies has decided to set some clear guidelines and provide support so that all field offices operate in the same manner. One of the first areas they are tackling is performance criteria for the sales force.

Case in Point: National Office Supplies, Inc.

Sally Scully is the regional sales manager for National Office Supplies, Inc. in the southeastern part of the U.S.A. She is an extrovert with a bubbly personality and a beaming smile. She is informal, direct and popular. Sally is a born leader and encourages cooperation across her team. Since she is in charge of sales, she doesn't think that performance criteria are important, after all the bottom line is how many sales the team makes. She generally ignores details and seldom writes things down. She looks at performance evaluations as pep talks. Sally passes out bonuses and rewards based on her feelings. This year there has been some serious grumbling about fairness. Several sales people are threatening to leave. There seems to be some concern about size of territories and the volume of sales.

Meet the Staff

David Rose is the sales manager in the northeastern U.S.A. He is totally different than Sally. He is an introvert by nature and very interested in detailed records. He keeps to himself. Generally, the team likes him. He uses the performance appraisals to meticulously relay details of targets, populations and performance data. It is pretty much a one-sided conversation. David talks and the sales people listen. If there are any questions asked they are usually by David and require a one-word answer. He focuses on mistakes and errors. He ticks numbers off in a box and this makes the difference in who gets rewards and bonuses. There seems to be some inequity because several employees that had maternity, sick and personal leave did not get much of a bonus.

**Exercise 1:
How might you
improve your
organization's
ability to support
collaboration,
communication
and sharing?**

1. Identify what practices are positive and which ones are negative in each of these regional offices.

2. What guidelines and expectations might need to be documented moving forward?

3. How might you augment collaboration?

    •   Individual

    •   Virtual Team

    •   Business

4. How might you augment communication?

  - Individual

  - Virtual team

  - Business

5. How might you augment sharing?

  - Individual

  - Virtual team

  - Business

6. What learning opportunities might you recommend for the individual, the team and for everyone in the business?

The use of global teams is common practice in the 21st century workplace. This has the positive effect of allowing organizations to bring the best players in the world together but the negative effects of eliminating proximity, removing or severely limiting visual cues, emotional detachments, and time and space constraints. It also puts a new light on operational knowledge within a company and across organizations. It forces people to share knowledge across the boundaries of distance and time. Operating virtually effects both unconscious knowledge and explicit knowledge and how it is perceived and shared. Knowledge sharing is always a challenge. Virtual environments pose even greater challenges for teams and leaders. Think of them as a three dimensional Rubik's cube where members can be in the same place, same time and same organization or they can be different on any of the planes.

Performance appraisals are only meaningful when they inspire, connect and contribute to success. Leadership and management are well-researched 20th century concepts. They are important factors in any organization's success or demise. The success of the individual can be linked directly to the success of the organization. Measures like turnover rate, employee satisfaction and learning tell us a lot about the culture and the long-term prospects for individuals to succeed. This can be translated from leadership right down to the individual and their ability to create and sustain their performance.

When organizations attempt to measure the performance of individuals it is usually labeled a performance appraisal (PA). Performance appraisal and performance appraisal systems come in many forms. Systems were installed and semi-annual and

Chapter 8

Mutually Agreed Upon Success

There's no magic formula for a great company culture. The key is just to treat your staff how you would like to be treated.
—Richard Branson

annual performance appraisals gave HR a way to feel important. They became hugely popular, although mildly effective, in the 20th century F2F workplace. By now, many companies have given up on the performance appraisal and thrown them out. None of it really translated very well to the virtual environment, which is unfortunate because in a virtual workplace interactive feedback it paramount to success.

The PA process calls for the alignment of desired individual performance objectives with larger business objectives. Sometimes this includes appropriate rewards to increase motivation. Too often this is a rote process that is casually and poorly done. Rather than being a path to mutually agreed upon success, it is an annual ordeal that is time consuming, irritating and ineffective. Employees endure it because it is tied to promotion and monetary rewards. Very little is really gained when the PA is little more than an empty exercise. The PA is not the only factor in organizational effectiveness. A sure way to tell how well the PA process is serving the organization is to look at the attrition rates.

Turnover results in the loss of valuable employees, as well as the costs associated with disengagement and hiring new people. Research supports that fact that there is a cyclic relationship between PA, rewards, satisfaction and motivation. Whether formal or informal, a feedback system free of judgment and opinions is essential for employee success. In a virtual workplace, feedback and mutually agreed upon expectations are possible only through interactivity. It's a two-way street. The leaders inform the virtual teams and the teams inform the leaders. Communication is the way performance gaps are discussed and eliminated. This interactivity is essential to meeting or exceeding business objectives.

Interactions in the virtual environment are intense and have more impact. People always say that the reason people stay in their pajamas until 2 in the afternoon when they work virtually is because they are so busy they don't have time to get out of them. Interactions can come fast and furiously at any time of the day or night. Tweets, emails and other messages that require a response bombard us. If you have not intentionally unplugged, you are open and vulnerable.

Virtual teams have a tendency to form and re-form constantly and have reporting relationships to different parts of multiple organizations. Teamwork is becoming even more important to success and networked leadership can span the entire spectrum of space and time. This makes leading in the virtual workplace a job that requires determination and commitment. Virtual team leaders need to establish communication channels and expectations that are clearly expressed. They also need to convey some mutually agreed upon ground rules that are adhered to and followed. This will increase the level of security, responsibility and interactivity. When people feel safe they are more likely to be open and communicate difficulties and challenges.

Often virtual teams are ad hoc. They are put together because of decreasing budgets, decreasing time and decreasing staff. The members lack the stability and intimacy to generate the interactions needed. They haven't really agreed upon anything. Members can come from all over the organization and outside of the organization. They are separated by time, space and distance. They are in a state of flux where membership on the team is constantly changing.

Here are some questions that might help us to determine how clearly those expectations are being communicated and whether or not we have established mutually agreed upon success criteria:

1.   Do you have a clear definition of what your role is and what you are responsible for?

2.   Is this true for everyone on the virtual team?

3.   Are you providing timely feedback to your team members? Do you have feedback time boundaries?

4.   Are you getting feedback in a timely manner from everyone you interact with? Do they respect your personal boundaries?

5. Are you evaluating and reevaluating the roles of the team members as you go along?

6. Have we mutually agreed upon what success looks like? How it will be measured?

7. Are you practicing FROG? Are the other people on the team?

8. Do we trust each other? Do you feel comfortable being honest?

9. Does our communication technology work? Are we keeping it simple and using it well?

10. What do our touchpoints look like? How often and what type of communication do we have with others? Do they have with us? Do they have with each other?

11. Are we including only those people who are appropriate in the meetings? Do we have an agenda? Is it meaningful? Do we follow it? Do we have enough meetings? Do we have too many meetings? Are things being accomplished because of our meetings? How do we know? Do we have mechanisms to take action? Do we follow through with action items? How do we measure it?

12. Are we reaching out with recognition and praise regularly? Do we celebrate victories? Even small ones? Do we have ways to recognize each other's contributions to success?

13. Are you clear on the team's purpose, mission, and objectives? The company's? Is everyone else? How are they being measured?

14. Are we all aware of cultural traditions and boundaries and time boundaries, and are respectful of each other?

15. Is all this written down or documented in some way? Is it available for new team members?

16. Are you proactively building those relationships based on trust? Is there enough interactivity to really share and respect the position of the others? Does everyone feel empowered to succeed?

These are just a few questions we might want to ask when agreeing upon mutual success. The exercises at the end of the chapter will help you build your own list. What is important is that we ask the questions, develop the approaches and stay open to asking new questions and finding new answers. Once trust is lost in the virtual workplace it is difficult to reestablish. Touchpoints is all about being proactive and building points of mutual compassion and trust. Touchpoints are a proactive process that establishes the necessary communication to be successful and measures the results. When we take responsibility for ourselves and set the ground rules for others and their interactions we can create success.

Often some type of social networking site or dashboard works well. There are many applications that do a great job of this and are easily available. They are, however, only as good as the people that use them. Don't get overly distracted by the technology. Instead put some thought into how and who is going to use it. How this will impact everyone on the team?

The classic example of misuse of this is the applications that give the option of receiving an update every time anything is changed or revised. Even with a team of 5 members, let alone 25 or 125, getting emails constantly gets really old really fast. Maybe a better policy is that each team member checks the site within a 24-hour period during the expected working day. If it is that important send a direct message or call only those stakeholders that need to be at the table. The volume of communication is not what is important. We want to focus on quality not quantity. We want to have a sense of how we are touching others, how the impact of our communication is impacting their lives. It is very important that we are aware of people's right to privacy and respect it.

Proximity is becoming a luxury in the 21st century workplace. Proximity impacts our ability to internalize emotion and our ability to detach. Conflict, crisis and miscommunication can increase exponentially in the virtual environment. Rumors, innuendoes and employee conflict are much more dangerous when we can't see faces and visual cues. Remember that unresolved issues don't go away, they go deeper. Personal attacks, vendettas and retaliation also have no place in the virtual workplace. Constantly reinforce there is no "I" in team and we are all in this together. Empathy, affinity and comradery among team members helps. It takes effort and it takes discipline. Stay on task and keep the conflicts and disagreements on that level also. Don't get personal with conflicts. Don't focus on when team members are working other than to set down time boundaries for personal lives and global time differences. Develop processes for communication and open channels that facilitate it. Make sure that people are getting the support they need to function with autonomy. If they need onboarding make sure they get effective onboarding. If they need a mentor or an apprenticeship then ensure that is what they get.

The purpose of the PA in a virtual workplace is to engage the disengaged. These need to take place frequently, be 360 degrees in nature and provide actionable feedback through interaction with other team members. They should emphasize what team members are expected to do and clearly communicate the impact of those expectations on the entire team and project or group. They need to establish clear and concise expectations and accountabilities and make sure that those are communicated to everyone involved.

Mutiny Virtual Style

Virtual teams operate in two dimensions simultaneously, the physical and the "electronic" space. These two are not mutually exclusive and can overlap. The fundamental guidelines for operation are very different in each space. Flexibility without losing control and autonomy without losing influence are constructs that are difficult for organizations and individuals to achieve. Time is probably the concept most highly impacted when times zones are varied and workers on other continents are involved. No one wants to get up for a meeting at 4AM because the rest of the team members on are on a different continent. But virtual time does allow 24/7 work and allows you to move things around the globe and between continents easily and effectively. It also allows individuals to organize their own time by choosing when to interact with the work and each other. Yet trust is at the heart of the matter and when virtual teams mutiny it is usually because trust has been violated.

It is difficult to know and accept when our team has turned against us. It is even more difficult online. When we can't see the plank and we can't see the prisoner, it is really hard to know what to do, where to turn and how to turn the situation around. The best thing you can do is to be judicious and build strong teams. However, this doesn't always work out. Even our best efforts can be misconstrued. Teams turn against leaders all the time and for all sorts of reasons. If a team member feels left out, not respected or not included they will return that sentiment. Online, it is very easy to feel unappreciated, unrecognized and underrepresented.

Recognizing when a team has turned against the leader or the mission is tricky. But it is always important to remember that people don't leave companies, they leave other people. A common sign that a team is on the verge of mutiny is that they just stop showing up. This is a true signal that the team has turned against the leader, lost respect and checked out. There is a reluctance to engage or spend time with the leader. They may not be hostile but they are very aloof.

The team members may appear to be pleasant but just detached. This response is passive and subtle. This shows that the team members have lost faith in the leader. Other things will take precedence, such as doctors' appointments, children's plays, visits from relatives, internet outages, computer problems, or any excuse not to show up. Alternatively, they show up but don't contribute, goof off and avoid team tasks. Gossip is a key sign that things are going downhill fast. When people lose respect for the leader, they look for satisfaction in other ways.

People who are frustrated and disillusioned want to be heard. Sometimes we need to bring in an outsider to help. We might be able to use a mediator and or a consultant from another part of the company. It depends on how deep this problem is and to what degree the team has checked out. The important question is what to do about a virtual team if we think it has gone off track. Doing nothing will only make matters worse. Either the leader or the leader's boss needs to step in and ask some hard questions, have some critical conversations and get to the root of the problem. If we can identify it, we have a chance to fix it. It is really important that the leader(s) realize that the mutiny began under their watch.

Leaders are not perfect; no one is. Admitting vulnerability and publicly acknowledging things are off track, what contributed to the problem, and what is going to be done to fix it is a good start. But it doesn't stop there. We must follow through. Admitting vulnerability adds to your power, it doesn't diminish it. We need to say thanks for the input, thanks for the insight and thanks for letting me know where things went wrong. Now, here is what we are going to do to turn this around. Ask for input and take questions with an open mind. By being willing to listen and deal with things head on you discourage gossip, and gossip can be extremely destructive online. You want to discuss the issues with people both one on one and in a public forum.

What we don't want to do is send out a survey and have the results remain secret. If we decide to use a survey, which is a formal indirect way of collecting information, make sure we publish and address the results. We want to ask for input and then show that we are willing to act to change things. The methods are not as important as the action. Keep the lines of communication open and rebuild trust. Trust is easily gained and more easily lost in a virtual environment. This happens because people are coexisting in two worlds without the constructs of time or space. Social bonding is critical on both a leadership and peer to peer level.

Trust and Virtual Teams

Everyone has a sense of identity. Carl Jung called this "individuation," which has to do with our sense of self. Self is concerned with what we will do and what we won't do. Our limitations, norms and culture help to define our identity. It is that innate sense of who we are and where our own personal limits, ethics and boundaries begin and end. In virtual space, identity is less well defined for some people. It becomes ambiguous and there is more freedom to de-individuate, or step beyond those constrains we use to define our sense of self. This is partly because the physical space, the body, the buildings and the rooms are stabilizing anchors. "You can only be one place at a time" no longer applies in the virtual workplace. You can have multiple electronic personas and multiple online identities. The anonymity of online is both a blessing and a curse. Information and identity are everywhere and nowhere. It all comes back to trust.

Many organizations support a culture that does not trust the worker to do their job and do it well. It goes back to industrial age psychology, of management vs labor, but really is founded on mistrust and control. Virtual workers require trust to make it work. Leadership needs to trust them and they need to trust the leadership. Virtual teams still require personal contact, strong relationships and that people get to know each other openly, honestly and well as people. This trust is built up over time and by social interactions and actions. Don't ever underestimate actions. Actions equal results. Once a virtual team starts working, trust depends on the results.

Virtual teams bring new challenges of social, economic, leadership and psychological challenges for virtual leaders and virtual team members. The illusion of supervision and control that was prevalent in the 20th century has to be replaced by a culture of trust and support. Virtual teams need to share work across the globe that is incomplete, and this requires new mindsets and attitudes based on trust. But they also still need personal contact, strong relationships and personal connections with each other as individuals (Kimble, Li, & Barlow, 2000).

When we evaluate performance in a virtual environment it must be based on mutual trust and agreement. Standardized forms and formats don't really matter. Feedback and clear expectations and how those will be evaluated does. Setting performance expectations cannot be a one and done exercise that is visited annually. Both the leaders and the team members must evaluate and revaluate at least once a quarter where they are and what they expect from each other. These evaluations must be ongoing and the results of these applied to taking action so that the organization, the project and the individual team members benefit from the feedback and move forward.

The administrative part of the performance appraisal is not nearly as important in the virtual environment as the developmental. Although there are still administrative realities in a virtual workplace, these need to be kept to a minimum. The performance appraisal needs to focus on the development of the individual. Both the skills and motivation of the employee need to be addressed and supported. Evidence-based conversations and new expectations need to be clearly stated, addressed, assessed, evaluated and acted upon. Learning in the virtual workplace is ongoing and should be incorporated into the everyday performance expectations for the individual. Learning and development is not an afterthought. It is a critical part of surviving and thriving in a virtual workplace.

Developing and supporting virtual teams requires a clear and mutually agreed upon set of expectations where roles and responsibilities and all the players' needs can be addressed. Both formal and informal communication standards need to be discussed openly and honestly. To avoid mutiny, leadership and team members must truly work on trust and avoid misinterpretation. A strong effort needs to be made by all parties, management and team members to connect. This will help set up performance management approaches that really work. Learning and development for virtual team members should include coaching skills, emotional intelligence and social interactions, technology, listening and relationship building. Communication needs to be multifaceted and address the individual as well as the business.

The virtual workplace is not about the technology, it never has been and it never will be. It is all about the people. People are supported by the technology and by other people. People feel secure and work effectively when they trust in each other and they trust in leadership. Training and development in the virtual workplace is challenging but necessary to assure organizational competencies and optimal performance. It is essential that leaders in the virtual workplace understand how to agree upon, establish, and measure mutually agreed upon success. Technology, although necessary, should be so accessible and usable that they become transparent to effectively getting the job done.

Case in Point: Bendz and Meeger Lighting and Staging Company

In 2016, Fred Meeger was ready to close his company. As CEO/Owner of Bendz and Meeger, Lighting and Staging Company, Inc., a design firm in New York, NY, he was frustrated. Most of their workers worked virtually, most of the time. The business was doing okay financially but his employees were suffering and complaining. Going to work was a nightmare every day. People had very low morale and were angry and resentful. "I hate this. I got into my own business to get away from this," Fred recalls. He heard gossip about how he ran things and about his personal life. His partner, Brad Bendz, suggested they consult someone before they closed the doors. Brad really believed this was a communication issue. Since most of their employees were virtual and not in the office, this might have something to do with what was going on.

1. What do you think the issues might be? How would you begin if you were the consultant? What questions might you ask?

2. What happens when people focus on being right all the time? How does gossip effect being able to meet business objectives? What solutions might you propose?

3. What role does leadership play in turning things around? How do difficult conversations help turn things around?

Case in Point: Style and Trends, Inc.

Joe Conner, the CEO at Styles and Trends, Inc., an upscale fashion magazine published monthly, had been hearing complaints about Catrina, a member of the executive team, for quite a while. He knew he had to do something because people were leaving the company. Good people. Catrina's direct reports thought she was too concerned with what Joe thought about her and not nearly concerned enough about them. They felt abandoned and isolated. Most of the complaints centered around Catrina blaming them when things went wrong and taking credit when things went right. The workers felt abandoned and unable to be heard. To make matters worse, Catrina was in the home office and most of the workers were remote.

1. What kind of policies might help in this situation? What can Joe do and what can Catrina do to turn the situation around?

2. Who is responsible for mutual success in this situation? How does communication play a part? How might judgement, trust and fear play into it?

3. Have you seen evidence of a similar situation? How was it or might it be resolved?

4. What do you need to do to build a culture where honest expectations are communicated and peer accountability is the norm? How might the group address poor performance and attitudes?

Exercise 1: Determine the Needs of Your Team/ Organization

If you were going to develop a simple survey to reveal concerns and issues:

What 10 questions would you ask?

1.

2.

3.

4.

5.

6.

7.

8.

9.

10.

Exercise 2: Lead a Virtual Team

What are the 3 most important things you can do to lead a virtual team?

1.

2.

3.

What technology do you need/have that will enable workers to remain productive in the virtual workplace: Security, Remote Support, Webinars, Smartphones, Audio/Video Conferencing?

Exercise 3: Assess Your Technologies

1.

2.

3.

4.

5.

Exercise 4: Assess Your Policies and Guidelines

What policies and guidelines do you need to put into place to manage a virtual workforce: Eligibility, Office Setup, Schedules, Evaluations, Reimbursement for Expenses?

1.

2.

3.

4.

5.

Measuring Performance in the Virtual Environment

Measuring performance is about communicating a vision and getting a buy-in. It sets discrete, measurable and attainable objectives at the team, unit and departmental level that relate directly to overall business objectives. The purpose of performance management is to improve business outcomes. Measuring performance in the traditional workplace is challenging. Performance management by definition needs to align with business objectives and other aspects of general management. It can't be looked at in isolation. Quality is all about service. Service is all about people. Separating performance management from the overall business doesn't work.

Good virtual performance analytics happen at least once a quarter formally and even more often informally. Using only yearly analytics in a virtual environment is useless. A performance review twelve months down the road is just not effective. Performance appraisals are traditionally used to identify outcomes: monetary, development, learning and personal improvement. This is a good place to begin but performance analytics needs to do much more. No matter what we call it, improving skills, motivation and performance is why we analyze it. We analyze it to support it, to try to fix it, to find out what we can do better. We design surveys, personal development plans and standards to insure quality. We analyze performance so that we can help people do it (whatever it is) better.

What we label as performance has changed over time because our understanding of what high performance is has changed. Technology and our methods of communication have greatly impacted this definition. Traditional performance analytics were

Chapter 9

Analyzing Human Performance

The biggest room in the world is the room for improvement.
—Helmut Schmidt

focused on top-down appraisals and initiated to assure directives. Today we have evolved to 360-degree feedback and to a flexible serviced-based approach. The focus of performance analytics in the virtual workplace is to confirm the vision, assure buy-in, and support development. Good performance analytics identify areas of improvement in the entire business process. They are a way of pinning down movable targets and communicating these targets so that they can be obtained. Performance analytics needs to be linked to something. Usually this is pay or promotion. Performance should not be taken for granted. Good performance needs to be rewarded.

Performance management is a process that involves setting individual, learning and strategic objectives. It is an iterative process. It is a systematic process. And it is an ongoing process. It is a process where individuals, teams and leaders look at progress toward goals and objectives. Success is gauged by the contribution an individual is making toward meeting organizational targets. To do this, a series of steps involving setting, measuring and evaluating these objectives is undertaken. Strategic objectives and targets are set for the organization and then different teams or units set targets that will lead to meeting the overall goals. Once these are set, then targets for the individual are usually established. Unfortunately, this is a top down, directive approach. Even if tasks are identified and activities initiated, it is difficult to monitor those in a virtual workplace. This is part of the reason so many organizations struggle with the concept of working virtually.

For years, performance appraisals took place between a supervisor and a subordinate and were based more on behaviors and personalities than on outcomes. Although interactions are very important in the virtual workplace there is no direct link between observation and organizational or individual success. Organizations need to implement an integrated approach that matches interactions with outcomes. The virtual workplace relies on teamwork and mutual buy-in. Together, goals and objectives are discussed and determined. There is a realization that not only meeting the goals but how the goals are met is important. How people get things done is as important to meeting those goals as what is accomplished.

Inputs lead to outputs. If there is a failure to meet a goal, what resources, processes, systems and protocols contributed to that result? Success or failure is not just the sum of individuals performing tasks. It is a combination of culture, technology, leadership and a host of other factors. Performance management in the virtual environment is not a matter of checking off boxes or filling in blanks. It can, however, identify staff development needs, gaps in processes and procedures and inadequate resources. Personal and professional development is challenging in the virtual workplace. It is not impossible.

Since the mid-1990s, performance evaluation has moved away from outputs and rewards towards continuous personal and professional development. This process focuses on identifying gaps in motivation and competencies and then providing the means to fill those gaps. Rating and labeling was labor intensive and ineffective. Individuals often didn't improve when scores and categories were used to identify inadequacies. This is exemplified in a virtual environment where group work or teams are usually responsible for the overall performance.

Top down is also ineffective in a world that is more open and much flatter. Virtual communication routes are more accessible and direct than what is represented in traditional organizational charts. Objectives set at the top and then sent out in a variety of directions have little effect. Do it right is being replaced by do the right thing. Rigid job descriptions tend to dissolve in a virtual environment and professional identity is being redefined. Working virtually is much less about moving up a corporate latter and being politically savvy and much more about making real contributions.

Organizations that are really interested in performance need to look at culture. In fact, organizational culture is a good place to start when evaluating performance. Organizations that are willing to look at silos, bottlenecks, and a general lack of cooperation and mission are more likely to have success with virtual workers. If the organization is willing to support and look closely at the needs of those people working virtually, there is a much greater chance for success.

Cost per unit is often used to benchmark performance. This might have worked in an industrial age where workers were thought of as just one more widget, but it is totally in appropriate in the age of the knowledge worker. In many sectors real costs are hard to measure and often are not measured at all, or not measured accurately. Hours worked is a very limited and unrealistic approach to measuring performance, especially in a virtual environment. The complexity of the environment and the performance task weight heavily in monitoring and evaluating performance. Performance evaluation begins with self-evaluation and planning.

This leads to new ways of measuring performance. There is a need to know how we are doing, both in the public and private sectors. If measures like performance indicators, ROI, and quality assurance do not do it, then what does? How do we look at performance and measure it both in the public and private sectors, profit and nonprofit, virtual and face to face work environments? There are many schools of thought on this ranging from checklists to blank sheets of paper, but ultimately it's best to get back to the basics: mutually agreed upon objectives, benchmarking and evidence-based research.

Setting up any kind of measurement system requires setting a target. Most organizations start with a mission statement and a definition of values. These values are translated into objectives or goals. The big difference between objectives and goals is that objectives are definitive and measurable. These are communicated to the workforce so that leaders are not only aware of the objectives but understand how their individual contribution plays into achieving the results. This includes their ability to contribute to the formation of the objectives. It also includes clarifying responsibilities, accountability, review processes and defining and measuring performance. The natural next step is rewarding performance and assuring improvement and progression for the individual and organization.

Planning for performance usually starts with a map that lays out where an organization is and where it wants to go. Usually these maps are set in a time frame of either a year, three-year or five-year plans. Achieving and measuring these results requires defining objectives that are measurable. Measurable objectives are set up with action-oriented verbs: What do we want to do, be or have? The more general the more difficult to measure so the more specific the better.

Setting up benchmarks is like selecting the starting point on a map. The term benchmark became very popular in the late 21st century and refers to a mark that surveyors made to set a beginning point. Benchmarking requires setting a unit of measurement and comparison. Performance is usually measured in terms of time, quality and cost. This has implications from personal benchmarking to industry levels where one business or organization can compare themselves to others in terms of best practices and where similar processes exist. The idea is always the same: identify a starting point then a target and measure progress towards or away from it. This allows individuals and organizations to evaluate progress. It also lets them know how well they set the target.

Is the target a measure that makes sense? Value management leans toward a measure of contribution. If benchmarking is going to be effective, and it really must be in order to measure progress, it needs to be reevaluated and redone at periodic intervals. When it is done and what is used is entirely up to the organization. But continuous performance improvement always requires reevaluating and refocusing.

Evidence-based research can provide invaluable insights into what is working and what is not. It takes time and it costs money. Any research is only as valuable as it is applied. Knowing something is wrong and refusing to do anything about it only magnifies the problem. Many organizations make the mistake of publicly sharing good results and burying those that are less than stellar. By not sharing them, they feel they are making them invisible and they will go away. If they are not shared, they will not affect performance. This is exactly the opposite of what usually transpires.

Competencies are defined by demarcating and determining base line levels of performance. Performance movement requires measuring that performance against predefined targets, ideally in meaningful ways, and then using that information to assure movement toward reaching them. Learning and development has shifted from a knowing to a doing orientation. Application orientation is based on competencies.

Evidence-based research and/or legal requirements set up competencies to get organizations to comply. This requires education programs and demonstrations of levels of performance. Periodical audits are done to assure compliance is being achieved. These audits usually use performance indicators and can range from individual workers to team or organizations. No matter what, performance indicators always measure against a prior assessment of problems or gaps in performance defined in some way.

Measuring performance in a virtual environment requires organizations to take a special and realistic look at their onboarding process. Onboarding is a formal and informal series of steps that familiarize the newly hired individual with the organizational culture, processes and procedures. Onboarding is especially important in a virtual workplace because the individual is removed from what is typically used as reinforcement of company values and norms. Onboarding familiarizes the employee with the company and often creates bonds with others in the same position. This bonding is very important to enculturation and integration. Virtual teams need to work especially hard to make the new people feel wanted, accepted and valued. They need to convey clear expectations and provide the necessary support. This includes processes, procedures, directories and services that support performance success.

A successful way to address performance is through an agreement, written and/or understood, that conveys key objectives, performance indicators and actions to be taken with in a defined period. Feedback from all members of the team is important in measuring performance in the virtual environment. Feedback should not be just top down but come from a variety of channels. Good performance management in the virtual workplace uses processes and standards as well as indicators to determine success.

Setting Performance Standards for the Virtual Workplace

- Start with the assumption that people can be trusted.

- Recognize that if you think the person can't do a good job you have the wrong person in that position.

- Understand that most people really want to do their best and do a good job.

- A system designed to monitor and punish will not motivate people to do their jobs.

- People never give their best because of checking and double checking the time they put in.

- Establish principles to be followed not rules that have to be obeyed.

- Establish touchpoints to improve performance, not just to increase contact.

- Establish a simple performance measurement system and monitor it for effect.

- Set ground floor minimums not pie in the sky ceilings.

- If the performance management system is difficult or meaningless or generates anxiety get rid of it.

- Make sure that the supervisors one level up and one level down had input into the performance measures.

- Make sure that the performance management system is relatively transparent and fits into the daily rhythm of the virtual workplace.

Monitoring performance in the virtual workplace is a means to an end. Virtual workers can save the company money, have a better work-life balance and contribute to lower energy consumption. Organizational and individual performance can only be evaluated in so much as there is a match based on a mutually agreed upon vision and trust. The relationship between individual performance and organizational success requires determining how much attention to focus on and what forms that focus should take. It takes an interrelated set of policies and practices to foster performance improvement.

Ignoring virtual workers because it is harder to measure performance is self-defeating. Supporting people to do the job well in a virtual environment requires positive communication and learning opportunities. Performance can be effected by information systems and inappropriate design of an organization. Some basic areas to address include competitive pay, benefits, equipment to do the job, levels of authority and responsibility, control, tools and organizational culture. Serious issues in any of these areas can create an environment where turnover is high and performance effectiveness is low. There is an old adage that says, "hire the right people for the job and pay them well." Virtual workers also need motivation to stay engaged and much of this comes in the form of feeling like they belong and are appreciated and supported.

Incentives can come in many forms. Clear performance expectations; clear criteria for promotion, stability and security; co-worker relationships; and a supportive, rewarding working environment are only a few. In this regard, virtual workers are not that different than traditional workers, only these things play an even bigger part in their loyalty and satisfaction. Performance management in the virtual environment needs to inspire and not be used as a punishment. Just like in the F2F workplace, virtual workers and supervisors need a process in place to deal with serious issues. Performance management should focus on positive factors and growth, not dealing with misconduct and retribution.

Autonomy requires self-direction, independence and accountability. The power is with the individual and comes from the inside out. It is not top down. It is not implemented by outside controls. It is not authoritarian or constricting. Autonomy is the ability to act independently and be responsible for your actions. Autonomy requires a bottom up approach to performance management. Organizations need to respect the individual and trust them if they are going to require autonomy. Performance in the virtual environment also requires clear communication of objectives and targets. Targets that are unrealistic, always changing and not assessable won't work. The virtual workplace is about planning and execution.

Measurement takes on new meaning and requires different effort. Clear communication that is consistent and relevant impacts outcomes. Sharing goals and objectives needs to be open, honest and done on a daily (or nearly daily) basis. Channels of communication can follow the organizational culture and structure but they must also emphasize each individual's importance and relevance to success. Both formal and informal communication channels are valuable and need to remain open. Closing any channels of communication for any reason can lead to higher turnover and poor morale. Both of those contribute directly to poor performance for individuals, teams and the organization.

Transparency and openness in an organization cannot be faked for long. Real concern for the individual and the relevance of objectives and agreed upon targets comes from the heart of individuals and organizations. If the heart is made of stone and there is no real compassion, concern and empathy, it will not take long for the true character of the individual or organizational culture to surface. Internal and external Band Aids like parties and outings or retreats will only go so far and will only be effective if they are meaningful and with purpose.

The ultimate measure of effectiveness, in any organization, is client or customer satisfaction. The main purpose of performance appraisals is to help an organization reach that objective. Internal and external pressures can impact performance and how it is measured. Decentralization, budget cuts, political power plays, market pressures, mergers and acquisition—the list goes on—can impact performance for individuals and organizations. Lean organizations are fine but too lean doesn't work. Asking individuals to do too much for too little reduces performance. Ultimately, it always about quality of service and meeting targets. How those targets are set, what they are and how they are measured may vary but one factor remains the same: Performance measurement is all about service quality. Ultimately, every business, organization and institution exists to serve a need. Performance is a way to identify whether or not that need is being met.

Heritage Bank is a large regional bank that has gone through many changes, mergers and acquisitions in the last ten years. Based in the southwest, they have banks in several states and a headquarters in California. The human resources group is dispersed and many of the employee assistance programs are administered online. The bank has experienced sound growth in recent years and has experienced an increase in turnover. The Director of HR is located in the main office but several assistants work at regional offices and virtually. They primarily advise branch officers on recruitment and selection, and do onboarding and compliance work. Typically, the Director of HR only visits local offices when there is a grievance meeting. The bank has some very broad guidelines on management but generally a hands-off attitude. Senior management at Heritage has taken the approach that as long as each branch is operating and performing adequately they are happy not to get too involved on a regional level unless they are directly asked to do so. However, the bank continues to grow and has changed from a small tight-knit organization into a larger, more bureaucratic one. Especially with more people working virtually, senior managers are keen to initiate a performance culture. Currently, not much is being done in this area. Performance appraisal are conducted annually but are not really taken seriously.

Meet the Staff

Alexa Skelly is a regional branch manager and handles banks in several states. She is a gregarious and extroverted person and is very well liked. She is mostly a hands-off manager and is much more comfortable with a face-to-face environment. Her style is typically relaxed and upbeat. Her conversational style is positive and she rarely writes anything down. She views performance appraisals as just more paperwork and not a big deal. Her attitude is that if people do better than they did last year all is well. She is a person who functions from gut instinct, not by referring to manuals and best practices. If she had her way, she would have those virtual workers back in the office. That way they could learn from each other around the water cooler and learn to talk the talk.

David Rosen is the other branch manager. David is an altogether different character than Alexa. He is quiet and reserved. He keeps to himself and is generally well respected. David views performance appraisals as very important and keeps detailed records on each and every employee. In the process, David reviews the findings against the objectives set last year. His performance appraisals are a series of question asked by David requiring one-word answers. These are recorded by checking a box. The questions are created by David. David takes the stance that performance improvement depends on avoiding mistakes. Performance can only be improved in the future by going over what was done in the past and avoiding those mistakes moving forward. David's employees seem to be defensive, nervous and generally uptight. David would also like those virtual workers back in the office because he is always asking them to justify their activities. He is never really sure what they are doing. He is the first to point out that he tries very hard to communicate very clearly with his employees.

1. What guidelines would you suggest so that both managers are using the same criteria to evaluate performance in the virtual environment?

2. What improvements in administrative standards would you suggest?

3. What suggestions would you make for employee development?

4. Is the goal of analyzing performance in the virtual environment to make better administrative decisions or to improve employee development?

5. In measuring performance in the virtual environment is it more important to look at objective or subject data?

Case in Point: Medsure, Inc.

Medsure is a customer-oriented business. It provides sales representatives for a variety of medical products and companies. It aims to offer products that provide value for the money but also high quality service. Medsure wants to grow their market. This involves keeping current customers happy and attracting new ones. Building customer loyalty is important to Medsure. Satisfied customers are the backbone of their business.

They service a diverse and rural market, mostly small pharmacies and other retail stores. Medsure has 30% of the market share in the Midwest and earned over 8 billion dollars last year. To keep on top of the market and gain new customers, the company needs to acquire and keep good sales representatives. Management, marketing, finance and sales—all levels of management—live by the same philosophy: "We treat each other with respect and everyone has an equal opportunity to excel, which ensures Medsure is a great place to work."

Meet the Staff

Brian remotely manages a team of 17 sales representatives. One of Brain's challenges is to make sure his team sells the right products at the right times. Usually he just lets his team loose and allows them to take the responsibility for achieving the right results, which worked really well the last time they got new products and he turned to the team for ideas. This produced team satisfaction and positive outcomes. His approach to management and leadership is laissez faire. He delegates responsibility. This usually works but not always.

Stephen manages a team of about 20 representatives. He has been with the company for over 20 years. Stephen tells his managers what he wants. He tries to persuade his team to accept his viewpoint.

Sometimes he will ask for input, but many times he just lays out the plan and expects others to fall in line. His area of responsibility has grown and so has his territory. Some of his representatives have never met each other. He is having trouble taking control and ensuring a prompt and coordinated team effort.

Victoria is a combination of the two. She is in charge of about 18 representatives and is more democratic. She will let representatives suggest ideas when it comes to selling new products but often tells them what needs to be done and when so that they can make their numbers. She sees her role as inspiring and influencing. She is not afraid to tell people "what's up" when she needs to and sell the idea, especially if it is a directive from corporate and she wants her team to support the initiative. She is constantly challenged by decisions, especially hiring new representatives. She has only been with the company a few years and her territory is growing. She is concerned the new people do not get the onboarding and training they need.

1. How would you measure success for managers at Medsure, Inc.?   **Questions**

2. What metrics might make sense (customer focus, personal integrity, drive, teamwork, developing self and others, managing change, loyalty, turnover, customer commitment, etc.)? Why?

Exercise 1: Create a Performance Appraisal

Remember that a performance appraisal is an analysis of the opportunity to perform and the organization's support for the individual to perform well. Truly analyzing results requires a format, not a form. It is a process that involves setting clear objectives and providing feedback. Use the example provided to start the process or identify a job and practices in your own organization. Pick a job that is virtual or has virtual components. Develop a format for measuring performance that makes sense in the virtual environment. How will you track performance? Analyze it?

- Role: Medsure Customer Service Representative (CSR)

- CSR Performance Tasks

	Telephone System
1	Answer inbound calls utilizing Medsure phone system
2	Verbalize company greeting on every call
3	Transfer calls utilizing Medsure phone system
4	Place outbound calls utilizing Medsure phone system
	Screening & Consultation
5	Authenticate callers based on Medsure policy
6	State confidentiality parameters with customer on every call
7	Conduct risk screening with customer
8	Conduct screening & brief intervention with customers
9	Coordinate urgent services after positive risk identified after screening
10	Follow up with customers according to policy
11	Apply solution-focused techniques with customers
	Medsure (CRM System)
12	Search for customer in the Medsure CRM computer system
13	Update customer demographics in CRM computer system
14	Locate product providers utilizing the matching application
15	Locate benefits and services listed in CRM computer system
16	Accurately quote benefits and costs listed in CRM computer system
17	Enter authorizations in CRM computer system
18	Apply invoice documentation format
19	Document summary of call in CRM computer system
	Medsure Website
20	Locate community resources utilizing Medsure website
21	Locate products utilizing Medsure website
22	Submit credit eligibility check utilizing credit system
23	Submit help request utilizing Medsure system
	HR & Personnel
24	Submit timecard utilizing HR system
25	Update personal information utilizing HR system
26	Request time off utilizing HR system

Exercise 2: Set Benchmarks and Measure Effectiveness

An ongoing evaluation and quarterly performance feedback is important for leaders to identify issues and gaps in performance. Evaluating performance in the virtual workplace requires setting benchmarks so that improvement can be measured. How might you measure and benchmark:

- Productivity

- Recruitment, retention and worker satisfaction

- Sense of community and belonging

- Value of the onboarding program to the virtual worker

- Cost reduction of overhead, communication, travel and power vs. subsequent savings

- Performance that supports business objectives, revenue, markets, growth

- Ability to support organizational needs

Most organizations don't realize that performance measurement lies at the heart of improvement. There are many examples that prove over and over again that failure to measure and determine cause and effect relationships can result in us accepting assumptions as truths. Data isn't everything but it is a good place to start when we look at performance in the virtual workplace.

From bloodletting to bumble bees to Garth Brooks, there are stories about failing to measure that prove how fallible humans can be. For more than 2000 years, the human cure for illness involved bloodletting. Today we consider this unthinkable. George Washington died of it and until Pierre Louis decided to measure it in 1850 and show that the practice did not increase recovery rates, it continued. It took a while for his discovery to be adopted. Eventually, however, his measurements lead to abandoning what was at best worthless and at worst a deadly process.

The scientific community has its flaws but generally embraces measurement and evaluation. Unfortunately, business is not as disciplined as science. Some businesses have excellent measurement systems for certain financial aspects. But for performance measurement, and particularly virtual performance measurement, most businesses are still in the dark ages. Like physicians in the 1100s, leadership is making decisions based on subjective information, innuendo, and beliefs about what drives performance that simply are not true. Sometimes they get it right. Mostly they don't.

When it comes to identifying relationships, nothing really beats measurement. Measurement works for identifying problems and well as opportu-

Chapter 10

Embracing Golden Opportunities

**Opportunity is missed by most people because it is dressed in overalls and looks like work.
—Thomas Edison**

nities. We avoid measurement for many reasons. One of those reasons is we are afraid of being wrong. Another is we are not sure what to measure. That's how the story of why bees can't fly came about. About 90 years ago, a scientist proved that bees can't fly. The measurement was based on the aerodynamics of the bees' wings. The bees' wings were thought to be a smooth plane. The scientist never looked under the microscope. The media got hold of the story and published it. Both the scientist and the media lived to regret it. Eventually each issued an apology, but the legend lives on. Many business decisions about workplace performance are based on the same kind of legends. This "Flight of the Bumble Bee" logic is often emotionally charged. People are supposed to be inspired by long F2F meetings, aren't they? I have heard this from managers of virtual employees more than once: "I can only control people when I have them under my roof. If I can't see them I can't influence them."

Winning these kinds of arguments can depend on making sure that performance data is interpreted and presented in a meaningful way. If people are going to embrace performance analytics for the virtual workplace, they need to be trained to understand the difference between data driven decision making and gut instinct. Aligning with business objectives needs to be more than reactive.

Performance measurement generally comes in phases. There is the initial phase where someone decides something should be measured. Then someone figures out how to measure it. Next the data is collected, interpreted and reported. Finally, someone reacts to the data by making decisions. If there are issues anywhere along the line, it can cause serious problems.

Garth Brooks and the surge of country music is a perfect example. In 1991, the music industry was in transition. Rock had dominated the genre for decades. Then this good-looking country singer named Garth Brooks hit the charts with hit after hit. Music industry executives were sure that rock was on its way out and country was going to take over as number one. But there was a problem that was based on data collection from an industry that was structurally in flux. Music had always been sold in stores that were not computerized but computers were what served as the data collection source. That source was Walmart. Walmart had a system for recording and reordering sales called the Nielson Soundscan system. As soon as someone bought a CD at Walmart, the system placed a reorder. The data was skewed because country music fans bought their music at Walmart and rock fans primarily used the music stores so nothing about rock music got reported. Once record stores went online it was clear that rock was as popular as it ever was. In the meantime, decisions to let go of contracts with rock bands cost the industry dearly. It wasn't long before we were looking at Napster and people were saying "Stores? What stores?"

The point is that kneejerk reactions to data are often Ill-advised. There is a process and discipline to performance analysis whether on an organizational, department or individual level. It begins with knowing that we are properly interpreting the data. Next, we examine the root cause of the results we are getting. This root cause analysis would probably have revealed that while Garth was good the data was skewed because of Walmart and rock was still king. Finally, leadership needs an action plan that applies over time. Whether measuring performance of a company or an individual virtual worker, it isn't one and done. Performance needs to be monitored over time.

The key to measuring performance is to compare. Without clear expectations, benchmarks and objectives it is impossible to answer the question "Compared to what?" The key is to start somewhere. There are plenty of measurement and evaluation formats out there. Some are better than others, but all have their points. The Balanced Scorecard, ROI, Performance Prism, Quantum Performance Management Model, Tableau de Bord and many more are popular.

What matters most is that we choose something that makes sense to the organization and DO IT. Customer needs and desires are the primary drivers of overall strategies, no matter how well that may be disguised. The primary driver of all training and learning is ultimately performance. This is what is of paramount concern in the virtual workplace too. Develop a strategy for measuring virtual workplace performance and implement it.

The ideal performance appraisal is a format not a form. It is a process that identifies strengths as well areas for improvement. It is a process for setting realistic, clear, well-defined expectations and measuring them. These expectations are for both leadership and virtual employees.

Performance appraisals have two primary functions, administration and learning and development. It is an iterative process where the results are applied at the individual, department and organizational levels. The standards applied to the individual virtual worker must tie in to the overall standards of the organization. There must be a feedback loop and a way forward. The administrative part of the process is more straightforward and needs to be considered first. The learning and development piece is more subjective and takes into account the individual's skills and motivations within a context. Jobs and expectations are ever changing and nowhere is this more apparent than in the virtual workplace. What is important is that the processes and techniques used to do a performance appraisal are evidence based, valid and reliable. The ideal performance appraisal may not be achievable but progress is possible.

Don't worry about too much detail or perfection. Measure what can be measured to a useful degree of accuracy. Think about the measures that you will use to measure performance. The depth, breadth and underlying logic of what a company decides to measure is a reflection of how well it understands and values the virtual workplace as a reality. What is important is that something is being measured and that this measurement ties into business strategies. Measuring does not assure that the business strategies this ties into will work. It does however give the individual, department and organization feedback about performance so that corrective measures can be implemented. Without measures, the individual's performance as well as the department or organization can be off track for quite a while before any problems are recognized.

Good intentions are not enough to assure success. Operational excellence needs to find its way into the virtual workplace. This means that measures must be logical, real world and applied. No one would argue that performance appraisals need to tie into business objectives. What is important is that this is applied to the virtual workforce as well as to those people in the face to face environment. Do you want 100% of your workforce working to meet your objectives or 50%? As more and more people work virtually more of the time this is a very real question. Even if they are working part time in the virtual environment, it is still important to incorporate virtual measures for performance into the overall strategy.

Measurement needs to cascade downward. What is measured at the top needs to tie into what is measured everywhere. The specifics might change because different functions need different measures and might require a greater focus on operations and processes. This can take some effort. But theories and strategies that are not operationalized are not practical. Determine what to measure and then set about measuring it. Measure something. Problems will crop up but then you can adjust the performance measures. The biggest challenge in implementing a virtual performance measurement system is usually organizational culture.

The virtual workplace requires people to change the way they think about work. It requires managers and supervisors to really think about workplace measures and expectations. It requires setting boundaries and limits. It requires planning and communication with intent and flexibility. It requires people to treat each other with respect and requires building highly functional but diverse teams. Change is easier for some people and cultures than for others. Leadership is critically important in this process. Leaders have to provide direction and support for the virtual workplace. They need to understand what is involved in virtual performance and determine what measurements make sense.

Effective measurement can be part of the organization, not an afterthought or an interface, but the heart and soul of an operation. Measurement is only the beginning. It is important that this translates into action. For some people changing and adapting is easy, for other is it not. Old beliefs, ways of doing things and habits of thought are very difficult for them to change.

Appropriate skills, knowledge, expectations, abilities and values need to apply in the virtual workplace. Developing and implementing effective virtual workplace performance measures requires effort and commitment. It also requires an investment into systems and procedures, but this is relatively small compared to the benefits. It can identify both problems and present opportunities. It assures that everyone regardless of location is on the same page and working toward the same goals. It allows the organization to attract and keep the best resources needed to achieve the objectives and goals. It allows workers to lead a balanced and productive life while understanding their contribution to the organization's success. It allows managers to take responsibility for meeting goals and provides them with measures that are objective and not based on guesswork. Most importantly, measuring performance anywhere takes effort.

There are certain steps to setting up any level of performance measurement. These include:

- Deciding what you want to measure

- Figuring out where you are going to get the data

- Collecting the data and getting it to the people who will analyze it

- Analyzing, summarizing and presenting the data

- Turning the summarized data into performance information

- Communicating it to the people who will use it to make decisions

- Using the information to decide what actions to take to improve performance

No matter what we are measuring it takes effort. Do not let this demobilize the efforts. We want to:

- Get started and set down a foundation for something

- Keep it simple to begin with and communicate the intent

- Get buy-in from those people whose performance we will be measuring

- Put some forethought into measuring and the implications of interpreting that measurement. What does it imply? What actions might we take?

Start where you are now. Getting better at measuring performance in the virtual workplace means searching for clues about what the obstacles are, how you might do things differently and what expectations you should have for these workers. This can translate right back into performance improvements in all areas. Once you have determined what is really happening, be sure to share it and develop an implementation plan for change and support. Determining what needs improvement is only important if you are willing to take the steps necessary to improve it.

Make sure you look at the root causes of the issues in the virtual workplace, not just the people involved. Do you have the systems, processes and interfaces you need for people to succeed? Look for those root causes and fix what needs to be fixed for good. Don't take the easy approach and put a Band Aid on it. Problems that are not solved will return more robust than ever. Performance targets need to make sense to everyone involved. If they are just numbers or ideas out of the air, then people won't take them seriously.

Remember that performance is about people and people deserve respect. The virtual workplace is much less tolerant of what should never have been tolerated to begin with: meetings that make no sense but go on and on; committees that procrastinate, prolong and create obstacles for no real reason; and teams that rely on group think and squelch innovation.

The virtual workplace relies on teams and teams rely on honest working relationships. Highly functional virtual teams rely on synergy. Virtual workers need appreciation from their team members and this appreciation needs to be conveyed. Intuition plays a big part in managing the invisible but needs to be backed up with clearly communicated expectations and measurement. Intuition is important but we all make mistakes and frame things based on what we know and believe. Implicit bias is alive and well in all of us. Clearly defining, communicating and measuring performance can go a long way to eliminating distrust and assuring results.

We are all human and all humans are capable of bias. It is more relevant in the virtual environment because bias is easier to fall into. Economists, psychologists and data analysts have categorized, named and labeled many forms of bias to predict and undue what comes naturally to human beings. The lesson from all this effort is really awareness. If you are aware that this can happen then you are already ahead of the game.

Whether it is weapons of mass destruction or subprime mortgages, we can convince ourselves of almost anything. In virtual performance analytics, we run the risk of making the evidence fit the objective instead of fitting the objective to the evidence. The virtual workplace is relatively new. It is unquestionably the future. How we construct our objectives for it must take into account new ways of working, new models of behavior and performance, and be much less reliant on preconceived notions about what has always been. When we get stuck in the theories we currently have we lose sight of what could be. Long meetings, boring committees and group think aside, the workplace of the future whether face to face or virtual will require a new way of working, and a new definition of efficiency and fostering innovation initiatives.

The workplace is increasingly becoming virtual. Old techniques for performance measurement just won't cut it in the new environment. It is not necessary to have extensive expertise of advanced data collection tools to do some basic performance analytics. The key is to start and the place to start is with the stakeholders. Traditionally, business leaders have had little faith in performance analytics with good reason. Much training, both compliance and non-compliance, is wasted. A great deal of it is low quality and not transferable to the workplace. This is set to change in the future because it has to. The successful businesses of the future cannot rely on the techniques used to improve performance in the past. Redundant and wasted efforts will not improve performance or business results.

The pace of life and business is quickening. We live in a world that requires us to keep learning. Analyzing learning and translating it to performance is a way to measure what is valid and reliable. Using scientific rigor to unlock patterns of behaviors and learning opportunities is the challenge that comes with the opportunity of "big data." The semantic web brings us more data than we have ever experienced. Being able to understand valid and reliable ways of making that data work for us is why we do performance analytics. It is about descriptive, predictive and prescriptive statistical approaches to unlocking patterns in the data. It is about setting benchmarks and discovering historical trends. It is about connecting business metrics to performance measures including retention and turnover, promotions, learning and development opportunities, quality, production, service, customer satisfaction, sales, revenue, market share, safety, product development, innovation and employee engagement.

Technology connects the virtual workplace and technology gives us an avenue to analyze performance in this new environment. Old measures like adoption and satisfaction have little value in supporting virtual performance. Efficiency, effectiveness and linked outcomes are a good place to start. As data becomes more available and evaluations more focused on supportive and enhancement measures, business will take more responsibility for results. There will be less manual intervention and less biased interpretations. The reality is that systems are much more effective at this than humans if the system is well design and administered. The current trend toward business intelligence systems that convert data into information and then make recommendations based on those results are a precursor to performance intelligence systems. Human performance and innovation are still at the heart of the workplace. "The real revolution is not in the machines that calculate data but in the data itself and how we use it" (Mayer-Schoberger & Cukier, 2013).

There are many models available for evaluation and they run the gambit from very simple to very complex. If the model is too simple it is impossible to discover cause and effect. If it is too complex it may never get implemented. Finally, business and the virtual workplace operate at a very fast pace and even within system analytic tools often the decisions are made without the consulting the data. Because analyzing performance sounds so overwhelming, sometimes we just don't start. If we can use performance analytics to determine what is missing and how we can support virtual workers, we have come a long way. Experimental design and determining real cause and effect are not always the only way forward. Many companies are not willing to fund experimental designs and with good reason. Business moves at the speed of light not at the speed of hypothesis testing.

As long as we have a good understanding, something is better than nothing. The main reason to measure performance is to help the business and the person. Processes, systems and gaps caused by inefficiencies can come to light. If there are cultural issues that need some work, evaluation can point this out as well. Ignoring the problem never solves it. Efficiency improvement is one of the best benefits that comes from implementing a performance evaluation system. This is true in the virtual workplace as well. We want to focus on interpretation, take the action required to improve virtual performance and not get lost in the analytics. Performance evaluation can be a valuable path for helping us make the virtual workplace an efficient and satisfying place to work. The key is to take action.

Conclusion

Managing a virtual workforce can be challenging. At times, it has proved to be overwhelming for many organizational leaders. It is a challenge that will not go away in the 21st century. The virtual workplace is here to stay. The opportunities it presents both to the individual and the organization far exceed the challenges. Aided by ever-better technology, the trend toward working remotely is gaining momentum and refuses to retreat. While some companies seesaw about their ability to embrace this new frontier, most would agree that the opportunities are there. Many statistics support cost savings in terms of rent, utilities and facility maintenance. Others indicate remote workers are more productive, report higher degrees of satisfaction and have a better work-life balance. Still others indicate that a remote workforce allows organizations to optimize talent and recruit the best people for the job from anywhere around the globe.

Building and sustaining positive relations is important in a workplace that is more complex, more disconnected and more time pressured than the one that existed in the 20th century. It is important that virtual teams collaborate and that leaders from all levels in the organization have the social and communication skills to bring people together, make them feel comfortable and value their contributions. The new workplace has changed the way we view place and time. It values results not just presence. It is also more dependent on technology, systems and processes that support success.

Virtual workers are more agile, more autonomous and usually more productive. When the structure of the organization is less hierarchical, there is more room for contribution and creativity. There is an opportunity to set goals, get buy-in and create a trusting and productive environment. This leads to innovation, improved life balance and personal freedom. From a business and operations standpoint, there is the opportunity to cut costs, meet objectives and attract workers from global workplace who have the best skills, talents and diversity. The virtual workplace allows companies to be more agile and more customer focused. Communication and mobile technology breakthroughs have given us the freedom to reinvent how we work.

Transformation and changes like this don't come without adaption and effort. Organizations need to train people in FROG communication, provide workers with understanding and support their needs at all levels. They need to create trust. Trust is created through mutual expectations and respect. We are asking people to work at increasing complex cognitive jobs. The age of the knowledge worker has changed the definition of the eight-hour day to one that is 24/7/365.

Leadership is about promoting different ways of thinking including trust and appreciation. There is a cost to the complexity of connecting using technology. This can be countered by developing close personal relationships and continued learning and growth. Virtual workers are loyal when they are appreciated and valued. They need to feel included. They need to know their contributions matter. They need time off and time for private lives. Leading, inspiring and measuring performance in the virtual environment is a two-way street. It requires the worker to have the personal skills needed for success. It also requires leaders to have clear communication skills and to develop ways to measure performance expectations.

References

Alford, H. (2015). The tyranny of constant contact. New York Times. May 17, 2015. ST 2.

Akinci, A. & Sadler-Smith, E., (2012). Intuition in management research: A historical review. International Journal of Management Reviews 14, 104-122. Malden, MA: Blackwell Publishing

ASTD Research (2013) Virtual Leadership: Going the distance to manage your teams. Vol. 5. No. 2

Baggio, B. (2014). The Pajama Effect. Coopersburg, PA: Advantage Learning Press.

Bailenson, J., Yee, N., Brave, S., Merget, D., & Koslow, D. (2007). Virtual interpersonal touch: Expressing and recognizing emotions through haptic devices. Human-Computer Interaction, 22 (3), 325-353.

Bauer, C., Figl, K., & Motschnig-Pitrik, R. (2011). Introducing 'Active Listening' to Instant Messaging and E-mail: Benefits and Limitations. Retrieved from https://www.researchgate.net/publication/229424196_Introducing_'Active_Listening'_to_Instant_Messaging_and_E-mail_Benefits_and_Limitations

Bell, B. & Koslowski, S. (2002). A Typology of Virtual Teams: Implications for Effective Leadership. Retrieved from http://digitalcommons.ilr.cornell.edu/cgi/viewcontent.cgi?article=1007&context=hrpubs

Bersin, J. (2016). Predictions for 2016: A bold new world of talent, learning, leadership and HR technology ahead. Retrieved from http://www.bersin.com/Practice/Detail.aspx?id=19445

Bollow, J. (2010). How Fast is your Brain? Retrieved May 14, 2016 from http://thephenomenalexperience.com/content/how-fast-is-your-brain

Brett, J., Behfar, J. & Kern, K., (2006). Managing multicultural teams. Harvard Business Review 00178012, 84, 11.

Campbell, R. (2011). The Power of the Listening Ear. Retrieved from http://www.rpdp.net/files/ccss/ELA/9-12%20ELA%20Journal%20Articles/EJPowerofListening.pdf

Christensen, C., Marx, M., & Stevenson, H. (2006). The Tools of Cooperation and Change. Harvard Business Review. Retrieved from https://hbr.org/2006/10/the-tools-of-cooperation-and-change.

Claxton, G., Owen, D., & Sadler-Smith, E. (2015). Hubris in leadership: A peril of unbridled intuition? Leadership, 11(1), 57-78. Guildford, UK. Surrey Business School.

Cullen, K., Edwards, B., Casper, W. et al. (2014). Employees' adaptability and perceptions of change related uncertainty: Implications for perceived organizational support, job satisfaction and performance. Journal of Business Psychology. 29, 269-280. https://doi.org/10.1007/s10869-013-9312-y

Dane, E. and Pratt M. (2007) Exploring Intuition and its Role in Managerial Decision Making. Academy of Management Review, January 1, 2007 32:1 33-54;

Duhigg, C. (2012). The power of habit: Why we do what we do in life and business. New York, NY: Random House

Evans, J. (2011). 8 Tips for Effective Virtual Teams: How to work with people that you rarely see. Psychology Today. Retrieved from https://www.psychologytoday.com/blog/smartwork/201104/8-tips-effective-virtual-teams

244

Ferrel, J. & Herb, K. (2012) Improving communications in virtual teams. Retrieved from https://www.siop.org/WhitePapers/Visibility/VirtualTeams.pdf

Gillies, M., Pan, X., Slater, M. & Shawe-Taylor, J. (2004) Responsive listening behavior. Retrieved from https://research.gold.ac.uk/2287/1/responsive_behaviour_cavw.pdf

Haid, M. (2010). The workplace revolution: Six steps to build a successful virtual workplace. Retrieved from http://smartwork.ee/wp-content/uploads/2011/11/RMVP_1010_Workplace_Revolution.pdf

Hammock, R. (2013). RIP Osmo Wiio: An accidently great communicator. Retrieved from http://www.rexblog.com/2013/08/24/49571

Heathfield, S. (2014). Culture: Your environment for people at work. Retrieved from http://humanresources.about.com/od/organizationalculture/a/culture.htm

Heathfield, S. (2017). How to change your organizational culture: You can transform your culture with conscious steps. Retrieved from http://humanresources.about.com/od/organizationalculture/a/culture_change.htm

Hemphill, L. & Begel, A. (2011). Not Seen and not heard: Onboarding challenges in newly virtual teams. Retrieved from https://www.microsoft.com/en-us/research/wp-content/uploads/2016/02/Not20Seen20and20Not20Heard20MSR-TR-2011-136.pdf

Hornett, A. (2004). Virtual work: Implications for human and organizational development. Human Resources and Their Development. Vol. II EOLSS.

Huppke, R. (2016). Smartphones throw a curve. New York Times. November 13, 2016. News. 31

Isaacson, W. (2011) Steve Jobs. New York, NY: Simon and Shuster.

Johns, T. & Gratton L. (2013). The Third Wave of Virtual Work. Retrieved from http://www.harvardbusiness.org/sites/default/files/HBR_Third_Wave_of_Virtual_Work.pdf

Kahneman, D. (2011). Thinking Fast and Slow. New York, NY: Farrar, Straus & Giroux

Kimble, C., Li, F., & Barlow, A. (2000). Effective virtual teams through communities of practice. Management Science research paper, No. 00/9. Glasgow, UK: University of Strathclyde.

Kirwan (2015) State of the science: Implicit bias review. Retrieved from http://kirwaninstitute.osu.edu/my-product/2015-state-of-the-science-implicit-bias-review/

Korkki, P. (2014) Yes, flexible hourse ease stress. But is everyone on board? New York Times August 24, 2014. BU 4.

Leavy, B., (2016) Jeffery Pfeffer: Stop selling leadership malarkey. Strategy and Leadership, 44 (2), 3-9. Somerville, MA: Emerald Publishing Limited.

Lloyd-Walker, B. and Walker, D. (2011) Authentic leadership for 21st century project delivery. International Journal of Project Management, 29 (2011) 383-395. Melbourne, Australia: Elsevier, Ltd.

Mayer-Schonberger, V., & Cukier, K. (2013). Watched by the web, surveillance reborn. Retrieved from http://www.nytimes.com/2013/06/11/books/big-data-by-viktor-mayer-schonberger-and-kenneth-cukier.html

McKinnon, T. (2013). How to build a great company. Forbes. Retrieved from http://www.forbes.com/sites/groupthink/2013/10/04how-to-build-a-great-company-culture.

Pepe, C. (2013). The secret to rock-solid conversation confidence. Retrieved from http://xperienceconnections.com/be-inspired/1-secret-to-gaining-rock-solid-conversation-confidence/

Rand, D., Greene, J., & Nowak, M. (2012). Intuition and cooperation reconsidered. Nature 489, 427-430. New York, NY: Macmillan Publishers Limited.

Rea, B. & Field, K. (2012). Managing virtual work "Business as usual." Retrieved from http://www.deloitte.com/assets/Dcom- UnitedStates/Local%20 Assets/Documents/IMOs/Corporate%20Responsibility%20and%20 Sustainability/us_ds_workplace%20transformation_11292012.pdf

Rogers, C. and Farson, R., (1987). Communicating in Business Today. R.G. Newman, M.A. Danzinger, M. Cohen (eds) Washington, CC. Heath and Co.

Ross, H. (2008) Exploring unconscious bias. Retrieved from http://www.cookross.com/docs/UnconsciousBias.pdf

Roye, A., Schröger, E., Jacobsen, T. and Gruber, T. (2010) Is My Mobile Ringing? Evidence for Rapid Processing of a Personally Significant Sound in Humans, Journal of Neuroscience 26 May 2010, 30 (21) 7310-7313; DOI: https://doi.org/10.1523/JNEUROSCI.1113-10.2010

Sasti, C. (2013). Effective Communications in Virtual Teams. Retrieved from http://www.open.ac.uk/business-school/sites/www.open.ac.uk.business-school/files/files/Virtual%20Teams%20-%20Carlo_S.pdf

Schmidt, C. (2014). Questioning intuition through reflective engagement. Journal of Moral Education, 43 (4), 429-446.

Simons, J. (2017). IBM, a Pioneer of Remote Work, Calls Workers Back to the Office: Big Blue says move will improve collaboration and accelerate the pace of work. Wall Street Journal May 18, 2017. Retrieved from https://

www.wsj.com/articles/ibm-a-pioneer-of-remote-work-calls-workers-back-to-the-office-1495108802

Sundin, K., (2010). Virtual teams: Work/life challenges-keeping remote employees engaged. Retrieved from https://esto5.esalestrack.com/eSalesTrack/Content/Content.ashx?file=9e2e8332-6b1b-4592-9dd2-4963636c94c4.pdf

Tonetto, L. & Tamminen, P. (2015). Understanding the role of intuition in decision making when designing experiences: contributions from cognitive psychology. Theoretical Issues in Ergonomics Science, 16 (6), 631-642

Tyssen, A., Wald, A., & Spieth, P., (2013). The challenge of transactional and transformational leadership in projects. International Journal of Project Management 32 (2014) 365-375, Strascheg Institute for Innovation and Entrepreneurship (SIIE).

Warkentin, M. (1999). Training to improve virtual team communications. Information Systems Journal. October 1999.

Watson-Manheim, M. and Belanger, F. (2002). Exploring communications based work processes in virtual work environments. IEEE 35th International Conference on System Sciences.

Whelan, J. (2013). Women in leadership: Understanding the gender gap. Chapter 4. The barriers to equality of opportunity in the workforce: The role of unconscious bias. CEDA (Committee for Economic Development Australia). http://dx.doi.org/10.4225/50/55763F6BA18EF

Zimring, F. (2000) American Youth Violence. Oxford, UK: Oxford University Press

Index

Bobbe Baggio, Ph. D.

Bobbe Baggio is currently Associate Provost of the School of Adult and Graduate Education (SAGE) at Cedar Crest College in Allentown, PA. Her area of expertise is the integration of technologies to enhance human performance including adult and workplace learning. She was the Associate Dean of Graduate Programs and Online Learning at American University in Washington, D.C. and was previously Program Director of the MS program in Instructional Technology Management at La Salle University in Philadelphia, PA. Since 2002, she has been CEO of Advantage Learning Technologies, Inc. a company that provides programs, products and research for workplace learning. She believes that technologies are here to help everyone and to enhance human performance.

Bobbe is the author of five books, an engaging public speaker, strategic advisor and educator in the field of instructional technologies and learning. She is a consultant in learning and talent development for a global and virtually connected workforce. Her expertise draws upon her experience as a Fortune 100 IT manager, 20 years of consulting experience, and her doctoral studies in instructional design for online learning. Examples of clients include The Federal Reserve Bank, Pfizer, Novartis, Johnson & Johnson, University of Pennsylvania, DOD, PASSHE, Merck, BMS, KPMG, Siemens, Ticketmaster, IMG, Tyco Engineering, Fisher, Christiana Care Health System, Cisco and Adobe.